Knowledge machines: language and information in a technological society

LANGUAGE IN SOCIAL LIFE SERIES

Series Editor: Professor Christopher N. Candlin

Knowledge machines: language and information in a technological society

Denise E. Murray

LONGMAN
LONDON AND NEW YORK

Longman Group Limited,
Longman House, Burnt Mill,
Harlow, Essex CM20 2JE, England
and Associated Companies throughout the world.

Published in the United States of America
by Longman Publishing, New York

First published 1995

ISBN 0 582 071321 CSD
ISBN 0 582 071313 PPR

British Library Cataloguing-in-Publication Data
A catalogue record for this book is
available from the British Library

Library of Congress Cataloging-in-Publication Data
Murray, Denise E.
    Knowledge machines : language and information in a technological
society / Denise E. Murray.
        p.   cm. — (Language in social life series)
    Includes bibliographical references and index.
    ISBN 0–582–07132–1 (csd). — ISBN 0–582–07131–3 (ppr)
    1. Computers and civilization.   2. Information technology—Social
aspects.   I. Title.   II. Series.
QA76.9.C66M89   1995
303.48'33—dc20   95–6900
                                                                      CIP

Set by 8 in 10/12pt Palatino
Produced by Longman Singapore Publishers Pte Ltd
Printed in Singapore

To Bill
for his conversations about information technology

Contents

whether technologically mediated or not, never actually possess that much vaunted and claimed moral and social neutrality.

Knowledge Machines is not, however, only or even chiefly about cybernetics and the control of the platform. It has a broader, and as we shall see, a more pervasive scope. As the first chapter identifies, the central questions to be addressed in the book concern the interface between human language and human literacy and technological innovations, whatever their sophistication. In particular, how technology impacts on our modes of communication, our socialisation, our structuring of language, our maintenance of social order. The sharp images of the book and its skilful unpacking of key metaphors indicate how problematic such an impact is: one such, that of the computer as universal machine or as a 'second self', is one through which to refract our experience and understanding of the human, not merely a catchword for technological advance. Not that computer-mediated communication can ignore the verities of communication itself: the issues of the boundary between the interactional and the transactional does not disappear with the advent of electronic mail, nor does the contest between language as structure and as organism. Nor does the massive introduction of computerisation in workplace communication disperse the social and discoursal issues investing worker-worker and worker-management interaction. Issues of the control and management of information are, if anything, made more sharp and to be contested. The quality of Denise Murray's discussion, however, is to canvass these issues, not as by-products of technological change but as essential and prior to the introduction of such change. What are the conditions of production and reception of technologically-mediated texts? How does technology affect communication pathways and the quality of messages? To what degree is the characteristic negotiability of meaning reduced by the propositionally-focused urgency of the electronically-mediated message? Or, equally problematic, how are the laidback emails of the apparently cosy one-to-one to be interpreted when in fact the message is a one-to-many management 'chat'? One key example for the reader to look for in Chapter 3 is the electronically simulated conversational encounter where the componentialising and reassembling of the 'typical' airline agent-customer conversation has a constraining, and on the customer a disempowering effect. Simpson's issue between the 'anthropomorphizing of machines and the mechanomorphizing of people', which Denise Murray highlights, spells out the struggle.

In this important focus on the social, it is easy to ignore the effect of computerising of communication on our general communicative capacities. Everyone will have experienced (or soon will) the disjunctive effect of answering machines and voice mail. What to say? How to message? As yet only linguists and discourse analysts have begun to focus systematically on the pressure such a medium places on our deictic capacity, on our control of tenor, yet all of us experience the voice-mail problems of inadequate referencing and the effects of such a medium on our interpersonal style. If computer-mediated communication will facilitate multiple discourse types concurrently, how equipped are we to manage and access such complex and interdiscursive talk? We know from research how complex and demanding remote communication can be; what effect will the computer as 'communication site' (in Murray's metaphor) have on further disenfranchising the communicatively disadvantaged? Yet, in contrast, as a partial balance, we know how those with severe communication disorder can have their lives immeasurably enhanced through the augmentative communication systems now available using the computer-as-speaker. It is the great credit of this balanced book that Denise Murray weighs up advantage against disadvantage, illustrates the issues clearly and tellingly, and through the discussion points at the end of each chapter, offers the debate to the informed reader. One characteristically far-reaching issue she canvasses throughout the book is the extent to which computer-mediated communication further disturbs the easy boundary between oracy and literacy. As she evidences, these are not dichotomous terms, nor are they best set at polar ends of some continuum as currently conventionally positioned. Much more than that, they constantly blend and merge intertextually as the contexts of interaction and medium change, making necessary not only our rethinking of the uniformity of genres but also putting at a premium the interdiscursive competence of users of the medium. Given that contemporary culture is increasingly communicatively hybrid and intertextual, one important pedagogic consequence is that we need to be careful that we do not find ourselves teaching a Fordist discourse in a post-Fordist workplace.

For many, the computer as utilitarian text-processor is the limit of their current requirement and their experience (though as Denise Murray makes plain, we are all expanding our involvement exponentially!). Fewer perhaps have speculated on the effect of computer-mediated communcation on their modes of composition

Acknowledgements

I wish to thank Chris Candlin, the series editor, whose patience, encouragement, and feedback were essential for the successful completion of this project. My greatest appreciation goes to my husband, Bill, who was more than a bystander in this project. He did more than encourage and be patient when I was busily reading or writing. He was an acitve participant in the project, providing invaluable insights into the effects of information technology, helping me to clarify ideas, to develop logical arguments, and to make the writing accessible. However, any errors in argument or fact are mine.

Processor power doubles about every 18 months; personal computers sell by the millions every year; networks and network services spring up all around us; upgrades to our favourite software come out two or three times each year; and new applications hit the market every day. The numbers may change; yet, through all these changes and developments I have seen during the course of writing this book, I have never had to change any of the arguments or issues raised. They remain, I trust, fundamental – ones that researchers, educators, and all citizens, whether providers, creators, or users of information technology, must address as we work and as we go about our daily lives. I hope that this book will encourage the thought and intechange we must have in order to make information technology accessible, secure, and usable by all, while ensuring our individual rights and freedoms.

ONE

Introduction

It is Saturday morning at Consumer Service, a busy discount store. A customer has come to buy some glasses she saw advertised on sale in their recent catalogue. In addition to the traditional order desk, which is a series of checkouts staffed by assistants who take the customer's completed order form and money, she spots a computer screen with the sign 'Silent Service' hanging over it. She has used this computerized ordering system several times at this store. Instead of standing in line and having an assistant enter her order into the computer, she can do it herself, thus saving time and preventing errors.

In front of the screen is a line of customers, but she decides it is shorter and should move faster than the lines at the checkouts. The customer using the computer is an older woman, who reads the messages and follows the instructions on the screen: she chooses to order, she then types in her telephone number (used to identify repeat customers), agrees that the computer has her correct number, types in the catalogue number of the item she wants to order, gets a screen displaying her order, types 'Y' to indicate that it is the correct information, and then the computer freezes. The only key that works is the green escape key that takes her back to the first introductory screen. She tries again. Again the computer freezes. She gives up, and walks to the order desk.

The man in front of 'our customer' begins his input. (He seems convinced that the woman could not get it to work simply because she was a 'mere' woman. Throughout her second attempt, he was impatient, peering over her shoulder, and looking frustratedly at other people in line.) His transaction also fails at exactly the same place. He turns to 'our customer' and says angrily, 'The computer isn't working'. Motivated by the desire to get the better of the machine and prove her superiority as a woman, our customer begins her transaction. Her input also fails. Like the previous customers, she is also angry. She has followed the instructions exactly; still the machine will not do what she wants it to. But, unlike the other customers, she decides to report it.

Since this is a discount store, sales clerks are as rare as diamonds; so she goes over to one of the checkouts and tells the woman checker that she can not get Silent Service to work. She is determined to find out what error she has committed and so waits until the clerk has finished with her current customer, and has called another checker to take her place. Our customer follows her to the terminal. The clerk pushes down one key on the keyboard, turns to our customer and says, 'People are always accidentally hitting this key and it stops the transaction from being completed.' This key, incidentally, is beside both the escape key and the return key, both of which customers have to use frequently during any transaction. To avoid hitting that wrong key is difficult. Our customer thanks the clerk, but suggests the store might have this problem fixed and so keep some of its customers. No reply. Our customer tries the terminal again. It takes her order. She goes over to the pick up counter and after some time, gets and pays for her order.

This store has not chosen a user friendly interface. Not only must the customer type all information, but the screen displays are language intensive with no graphics. At a different store, Sears, information is displayed on a screen and the customer touches the screen to make choices. But there is a difference, the Sears system is for picking up goods already ordered by telephone while the Consumer Service system is for ordering merchandise to be collected almost immediately. However, there is no technical reason why the Consumer Service system can not use a touch sensitive screen, thereby saving the customer from typing errors or why they can not present the online information more attractively, or even just fix the keyboard to prevent the lock up of the entire system by hitting one key. This system defeats the purpose, which presumably is to reduce the number of employees and thus lower costs; in fact it actually irritates customers and risks driving them away in frustration!

I need to renew my Australian passport and so call the Australian Consulate-General in San Francisco – a long-distance phone call. The call is answered by a menu message machine, which begins 'Thank you for calling the Australian Consulate-General. If you know the extension you want, press it now. For information regarding visas, immigration, Australian passports, trade and customs, press 1. For consulate location and hours of operation, press 4. For an operator, press 0.' Since I want to renew my passport, I press 1 and receive a further menu, saying 'For tourist visas, press 1. For limited stay and working temporarily in Australia, press 2. For immigration, press 3. For business immigration, press 4. For birth registration, press 5. For renewal of lost or expired Australian passports, press 6.' So, I press 6 and hear 'You have reached the issuing office of Australian passports. If you want a passport application form, leave you name and address and one will be mailed to you. If you want a personal appointment, leave your name and telephone number and your call will be returned. If you want to speak to an operator, press 0. To leave you name and address, begin at the sound of the tone.' I left my name and address and a few days later an application form arrived in the mail.

For me, this was an efficient way to get the form. I did not have to stay on hold or get a constantly busy signal. Unlike many other menu systems, I always had the option of pressing 0 to get a live human being. In addition, the female voice spoke clearly and quickly so that I did not have to wait long to hear the entire menu.

Stanley and Ben are in the same fifth-grade class and have been together at school since first grade. They are friends at a distance, but belong to two different worlds. Stanley is another math whiz and always has been. He is the child of academics and describes himself in terms of his technical interests. He has been fixing radios since he was five, is deeply interested in electronics and circuitry. He wants to be a patent lawyer when he grows up, and his reasons are 'technology-driven'. 'You get to learn the latest stuff about machines and about computers, stuff you would need to know anyway.' Ben is in the 'other' culture, a dancer. When school is over he is off to dancing lessons or rehearsals. At eleven years old he is already a professional.

Stanley and Ben developed a collaboration . . . to produce a program that would choreograph a dance of sprites on the screen. Each collaborator brought to the task something the other did not have. Ben brought his sense of form, of movement, and his already well-stocked repertoire of dance routines. But to translate these for the computer required Stanley and his repertoire of programming tricks.

(Turkle 1984, p. 128)

The collaboration between Stanley and Ben illustrates the best in education and the application of technology – each child brought his own contribution to the task and, in the process, was able to appreciate a different world view. But, what about other uses of computer technology, uses that may invade our lives, either with too much information, or by exposing us and our world to danger?

It is 9:30pm and Bill has just arrived home after a three-day business trip to the East Coast. Although on business, he was at a conference center that had no terminal links to the IBM network. He logs on to our home personal computer (PC), connects to his mainframe at work, and calls up the screen of electronic mail (e-mail) that has arrived during his absence.

I hear the angry mutterings and cursings as far away as the kitchen – '95 notes – my god, it'll take me all night to read them'. In just three days, Bill's e-mail box has received 95 new notes, ranging in length from one-line reminders to many-paged memos; from urgent action items to 'junk' mail.

Computer telecommunications free us from the time and spatial constraints of more traditional human conversation, but at a cost. Junk e-mail proliferates. People copy all and sundry so they can not be accused of not informing workers or managers. Others send all manner of documents and notes, in case they might be of some interest to the recipient.

Newspaper columnist Art Buchwald, in a 1988 column in the *San José Mercury News*, tells of an imaginary, but not improbable, tale of the White House trying to contact Gorbachev via the new computer 'hot line'. Someone has made an error and World War III is about to start. After connecting with the operator at the computer keyboard at the United States end of the hot line, and asking for Mr Gorbachev, the President is asked for Gorbachev's first name, then his Social Security Number, but the operator can not find a listing. She tries rerouting the request. The computer gives her ballet ticket information, then airline information. She then tries the online telephone directory, but gets instead Raisa Gorbachev's credit card data. After further misconnections and miscommunications, the President talks to Gorbachev, who has been on the telephone line the whole time. The President reassures him that different operators will run the Star Wars system.

These examples of our interactions with computers as we go about our everyday lives tellingly illustrate the type of knowledge we need to have just to access the information we need. They also demonstrate the need for more research on the human–machine interface so that users face minimum frustrations and potentially disastrous errors in their interactions with these computers. We need to master this resource. What do we need to do this successfully? Certainly we need to be literate – *truly* literate, not merely *computer* literate. Even with Sears' touch screen system, the customer must be functionally literate. With Consumer Service's language intensive display, we need to be highly literate. And yet, even in countries with compulsory public education for eight or more years, literacy levels are declining. How will/can such people function in this information society? We also need to be computer literate, but what exactly does that mean? How transparent should the technology be? Which metaphor is better, the piano or the automobile? Those who choose the piano metaphor claim that since we can not play a Beethoven concerto immediately, we should not expect to be able to use the computer immediately. Those who choose the automobile metaphor say that we only need to know how to *drive* the computer and reach our destination; we do not have to know what is under the hood. Even if we accept the car analogy, learning to use a computer competently takes time. It takes 10 to 20 hours of training to learn to drive a car with minimal competence and about 40 hours, plus ground school, to fly a plane.

Luehrmann, who probably invented the term 'computer literacy' while he was director of computing at Dartmouth College in the early 1970s, has recently claimed that 'Computer literacy allows a different translation [of verbal and mathematical codes], into a code that permits general and realistic representation of a process, which is easily adapted to new circumstances' (McCorduck 1985, p. 219). This definition allows for different levels of literacy. Not everyone will want to be able to play Beethoven; but we may all have to drive a car. The challenge for system designers then is to determine which computer applications require a minimum acquisition load and which can suitably require more mastery of computing. As we move through this book, we will see that a goal of many computer scientists, especially those working in artificial intelligence, is to develop computers that appear to respond like humans. There are others, more pragmatic, who see this goal as unattainable and therefore strive for systems that 'let people operate effectively in a systematic domain that is relevant to human work' (Winograd and Flores 1986, p. 175).

This book argues that technology both transforms and is itself transformed by society. It not only transforms what we do, but also how we construct our world. This claim is not new, nor does it apply only to that technology brought about by the silicon chip – computer technology. Previous technological innovations (such as the printing press) have affected society, people's ways of interacting, and discourse itself. In turn, as we use technological innovations in both planned and unplanned ways, we create changes and advances in the technology itself. Yet, the history of the development of other technologies shows us that the technology itself is not sufficient to create changes. For all the hype about how computers will change organizations, human communication, and the very way we think, many changes have been superficial.

Indeed computer technology can be, and sometimes is, co-opted by those in power to maintain the status quo and prevent change. Critical to any change is not just who has access to information, but who has the capacity to *use* the information.

Since this book focuses on the interaction between language, society, and technology, the discussion is confined to those technological innovations that involve language centrally. All technology in some way involves language, but often peripherally. For example, the automobile has led to a register of car language, to the use of icons for dashboard switches or road signs, computerized voice, telling the driver or passenger to 'Please fasten your seatbelt', and metaphors that leak into everyday language (e.g., 'not firing on all cylinders').

While such linguistic innovations are of interest, this book focuses on areas of technology in which language is central to the operation of the technology, or the technology is devised as a vehicle to facilitate discourse among humans. Technology that comes immediately to mind for most lay people would be computers and the telephone. While computers pervade the marketplace and our daily lives, many are invisible, that is, the user does not need to know anything about computers in order to function successfully. Consumers need have no computer literacy (or even know that computers are involved) in order to operate electronic ovens, multifunction watches, or even a fuel-injected car. In fact, as one manufacturer said in 1983, 'The future lies in designing and selling computers that people don't realize are computers at all' (*Time*, 3 January 1983, p. 24). This is the 'ubiquitous computer', which computer scientists are predicting for the future. Technologies (e.g., literacy) often become part of the fabric of society, so much so that, although present in every aspect of our lives, their presence is not noted. Information technology is not yet ubiquitous – indeed, the computer interface that people have to use includes often opaque symbols or complex commands that seem unrelated to the purpose of using the machine. And, it is just this intrusion of a new way of communicating information that affects language and social processes. When the computer does become ubiquitous, it too will create new ways of using language; but that time has not yet come, although the signs and directions already visible will be discussed in this book. The argument and discussion around computer technology will focus on the current discernible applications.

The other focus is on information technology, or what is also called computer science. All computer applications in some way transform information. The automobile computer transforms information that a seatbelt is not fastened into digitized code. This code is then read by the computer which is programmed to respond with another digitized code. This next code is transformed into a voice saying 'Your seatbelt is not fastened'. However, the focus here is narrower, a discussion of those uses of the technology through which humans need to provide or access information. Thus, this book does not deal with automation of service industries such as McDonald's, but it does deal with the automation of American Airlines' reservation clerks since the public calls them to get information. The quantity and quality of information available is restricted by management standardizing and automating their agents' conversations with customers. In other words, this discussion will focus on language and information-intensive computer technology in which the technology is not completely hidden from the user.

It is vital to discuss the interaction of computers, language and society. Our future work and social lives will depend on how we develop and use information technology. With the introduction of the personal computer (PC) more than a decade ago, the use of computers moved from being the province of computer programmers to a more universal tool, which is reflected in the fact that the United States has approximately one PC for every seven people. However, the distribution is uneven – PCs are more likely to be found in the homes and schools of people in higher socioeconomic brackets. But, people at all levels of society are finding they need to work with some form of computer to shop, to bank, to do their jobs, and to communicate with others, communication being one of the major uses of information technology. Peter Lyman (1994), claims that the NSFNET (National Science Foundation Network) is used primarily for communication, not computation, the task for which computers were originally designed. 'Simply put, the computer and the science surrounding it have everything to do with our lives, from new forms of art to new forms of medicine, from new ways of work to new ways of communicating' (McCorduck 1985, p. 91).

The central questions raised by this discussion will be

1. How does the nature of human language constrain/facilitate such technological innovations? How does this affect social interactions and organization?

2. How does the structure of the technology provide models for human language and interaction? How does this change the way we see our humanness and social being?
3. How does human language adapt to the technology? What effect does this have on social processes? And on social-psychological processes?

To answer these questions, the book argues that implementations of information technology have been less than successful, that society has not been receptive to these innovations because they were based on 1) inappropriate or underdeveloped models of human communication and information management or 2) metaphors applicable to earlier technologies that may no longer be useful for these new technologies. Indeed, it is the very metaphor of the machine itself that has inhibited many people. In the last century Lady Lovelace warned against limiting our thinking of what Babbage's machine (the computer) could do just because it used arithmetic notation. Yet, our thinking has been limited by this metaphor, reinforced by computer companies who advertise the speed at which calculations can be done, speeds which are so far beyond our human comprehension that we are awed and fail to think critically about what the computer can do for us. Certainly, throughout this book, we will be reminded of the speed of the computer because it is precisely that characteristic that is so often touted as its *raison d'être*. While the computer at its most primitive level does make calculations, it is far from being a fast calculating machine – so much so that many writers have rejected the 'computer' metaphor. Alan Turing, the British computer scientist, was the first to call it the 'universal machine' because it can be programmed to perform whatever tasks we want. Sherry Turkle (1984) calls it 'the second self' because she sees the computer as a mirror that evokes questions about what is mind and what it is to be human. This is one of the basic questions in the artificial intelligence debate – if computers can exhibit artificial intelligence, what does it mean to be human? Each metaphor reveals our search for understanding of the computer, its functions, and its role in our lives.

To answer the guiding questions in a principled way, I have had to make theoretical distinctions about language, society and technology that are blurred in actual real-life situations. However, these distinctions provide a framework for organizing the web of interconnectedness among language, society and technology. Thus, the book itself and the theoretical framework is divided into chapters that mirror some of the essential ways humans work with language and computers. It begins by looking at the way humans process communication. This will provide a background for discussing the way computers organize information and use language – the focus of the book. For the titles of the chapters discussing the use of computers, I have used metaphors to describe computers. As Lakoff and Johnson (1980) show, we use metaphors to help us understand the world, but these metaphors also take on a life of their own, shaping the very way we think about things. If we talk about a marriage using journey metaphors (e.g., 'going off the rails', 'on track'), we will see marriage as linear, with a beginning and an ending, with each day taking us closer to the end of the journey. So often metaphors hide the very assumptions that need to be uncovered to develop a new view of the phenomenon. With this caveat in mind, I still use metaphors with caution because they are in common parlance and they show what our current society considers salient features of the computer. At the same time, I want to uncover the assumptions underlying these metaphors, assumptions that need to be questioned before we can search for a new paradigm for studying and understanding computers and society.

Thus, the chapters include the computer as worker, as phone message service, as mail service, as text processor, and as knowledge broker. Although all the other metaphors are encountered in the workplace, there is a separate chapter on computers as workers since it is in this domain that most people have their major encounters with information technology. In each chapter, discussion will focus on how language and society are impacted and impact the technology. The final chapter raises issues of privacy and control, issues that linguists, computer scientists, and others interested in the social life of humankind need to address to ensure the technology is empowering for all.

Throughout the text, I use first person singular to describe events I have witnessed and also to indicate what are my own arguments. At other times, I also use the inclusive 'we'. I realize that this can be used by writers to seduce readers into agreeing with them. That is not my intent. Rather, in such sections, I want readers to join with me in exploring an issue and taking a position. The text also contains a number of illustrative scenarios such as the ones in this introduction. My hope here is to make the issues alive for readers and also help them relate the argument and ideas to experiences they may have had with computers. For each scenario we need to ask:

1. What model of *communication* is this knowledge machine application based on?
2. What model of *information handling* is this knowledge machine application based on?
3. How similar is the *communication* to that used by humans in their non-technologically mediated interactions?
4. How similar is the *information handling* to that used by humans dealing with information without technological intervention?
5. How might this *communication* and *information handling* affect the way we communicate and handle knowledge without technology?
6. Is the application based on metaphors for earlier technology? Are such metaphors relevant here?
7. What implications does this application have for the social interaction of humankind and what implications does it have for maintaining or altering the social order?

SOME DEFINITIONS

I use *technology* to include both the machines *and* the ways they are implemented. Thus, for example, a personal computer used with a spreadsheet or with a wordprocessor constitutes two different technologies.

- I use *information technology* to mean the 'machines, artifacts, and procedures used to gather, store, analyse, and disseminate information' (March and Sproull 1990, p. 144).
- I use *computer* to refer to any programmable machine, that is, a machine whose instructions for use can be altered.

HOW TO USE THIS BOOK

Chapter 2 provides the background information about language and information processing for understanding how the use of computers is similar to or different from our more common communication and information handling. Chapters 3 to 8 examine different roles the computer plays in our lives. Although the ordering of these chapters has been made deliberately, they can be read independently. Each chapter concludes with discussion questions and suggestions for activities the reader may engage in to better understand the issues in the chapter. Where applicable, chapters also include an annotated list for further reading.

TWO

People communicating

A student walks up to the department office and asks the secretary, sitting at the reception desk, 'Do you know where Professor Murray is?' The secretary answers, 'Yes'. The student, confused, says, 'Oh, thanks', and walks away.

This book is about the social construction of information technology and therefore involves the way we communicate. So, in this chapter, I will examine the linguistic concepts that we will need to explore the way computers organize information and human communication. The discussion will be brief, identifying only those characteristics that are most salient to the theme of the book. The chapter will focus on two areas: how people interact using language, and what we know about the sociocultural practice of literacy. The former is vital to our understanding of how language, society and technology intersect. Many of the conventions of linguistic interaction are implicit to the user, but shared by all users of the language. Without such shared rules, our interactions would breakdown. Indeed, it is only when a speaker (or listener) flouts one of the unwritten rules, that we are even aware there *are* rules, as in the example above. The student was so taken aback that she walked away, unsure of what had actually taken place. After a few minutes, however, she returned and re-asked her question because she realized the secretary had violated one of the conventions of requests for information. The secretary this time responded, 'Yes. She's in Room 230.' This particular secretary enjoyed flouting conventions to see how people responded!

Language use is also a cognitive function of the human brain, building on world knowledge and linguistic knowledge. Such an understanding is important in the field of artificial intelligence. However, this book takes the stance that

Language is as it is because of the functions it has evolved to serve in people's lives; it is to be expected that linguistic structures could be understood in functional terms. But in order to understand them in this way we have to proceed from the outside inwards, interpreting language by reference to its place in the social process. This is not the same thing as taking an isolated sentence and planting it out in some hothouse that we call a social context. It involves the difficult task of focusing attention simultaneously on the actual and the potential, interpreting both discourse and the linguistic system that lies behind it in terms of the infinitely complex network of meaning potential that is what we call culture.

(Halliday 1978, pp. 4–5)

Literacy, the second focus of this chapter, is important because the computer is often likened to the printing press. In 1986, a three-page headline in the *Wall Street Journal* (21 February, pp. 11–13) announced that 'In 1455 Gutenberg brought the miracle of printing to the civilized world . . . 531 years later, Apple brings it to the civilized desktop.' This analogy has become an accepted myth in this technological era. To understand that it is indeed a myth, we need to examine the history of literacy practices in detail, which this chapter will do.

PEOPLE INTERACTING THROUGH LANGUAGE

What have linguists and others discovered about the social semiotic of everyday use of language between people, as they talk and write? This discussion will set the scene for later chapters, in which I will show how the use of information technology is altering many of the conventional ways we use language in going about our lives. A number of different disciplines have studied language and its use for communication among people. Theories abound. Here, I will focus only on those aspects of communication that are salient in communication via or with computers.

Since interaction with and via computers includes both spoken and written language, we need to examine the ways people communicate with each other in spoken and written discourse. What is most remarkable about human communication is that we strive to make sense of discourse that is fragmented, contains grammatical errors, and appears unrelated. For example, most people have no difficulty interpreting the following short telephone conversation:

A: Is Jerry there?
B: Yes, I'll get him for you.

Although the caller does not request to speak to Jerry, the listener knows that the question is more than just a yes/no question and that if she only responded 'yes', she would be considered to be behaving abnormally. Similarly, most people have no problem interpreting the following text, despite the grammatical errors and apparently unrelated facts (taken from an essay by a non-native speaker of English):

> Social rituals are an important part in human life. Any religion has its own special ritual ceremonies. The social rituals have been transferred from older generation to the other one. Depend to the country, the social rituals carry out at least the social class in the society. Among the oriental people, the social rituals have been respected as a moral life. They can save money in eating, clothing but they never save it in social ritual ceremonies.

To understand language in actual use, we must of course understand grammatical structure, but to interpret it, we must know far more – it is this additional knowledge that is the focus of the study of discourse. In the literature, written language and spoken language are referred to variously. For the sake of clarification in this book, I will use discourse to refer to language in use and text to refer to the actual product of discourse that linguists study. In this chapter, then, I give a general overview of discourse in society, covering those characteristics that are relevant to the later discussion of computers and language, as follows:

1. *Context of situation*: the interrelationship between situation and language, how the situation affects discourse and how discourse itself affects the situation.
2. *Functions of language*: the primary roles of language in communication, what people use language to do in their discourses.
3. *Cohesion, coherence and schemata*: the way discourse is structured to show the relationship between ideas and the way we interpret discourse to make sense of it.
4. *Conversation*: the way spoken interaction is organized and structured.
5. *Speech event*: the specific culturally determined activities that are governed by cultural norms for the use of speech.
6. *Public and private language*: the social controls on where language can be used.

Context of situation

Language varies depending on the context of its use and on charac-teristics of the user. Most of us are more aware of language differences due to user characteristics than due to differences of use. Speakers from different regions, different classes, different eth-nic groups, of different gender, and of different ages speak differently. Of more importance in the examination of communica-tion with and via computers is the notion of variation resulting from use, that is, from the choices individuals and groups make to achieve their particular purposes. Such variation has been called register by British and Australian linguists (e.g., Halliday 1978) and speech style by American anthropologists (e.g., Hymes 1972). How are people's uses and choices altered as they try to achieve their particular purposes using computers?

Components of context

To relate speech styles or registers to the context in which they occur, researchers have developed the concept context of situation, first introduced by the anthropologist Malinowski (1923) as a means of explaining how the totality of a culture affects the lan-guage used for a particular speech event. The linguists Firth (1957) and his student, Halliday (1978) developed taxonomies of context parameters that influence the language used, that is, the register. While there are competing taxonomies (Hymes, for example, lists eight, which he identifies under the mnemonic SPEAKING; Halliday lists three metafunctions – field, mode and tenor), all agree on three broad categories:

1. audience factors
2. topic factors
3. setting factors.

Halliday's taxonomy best describes the context for communica-tion with and via computers:

- *Field*, which refers to the process or activity within which the language is embedded and the role that language plays within the activity. Thus, field includes more than topic; it includes orientation to the topic. For example, in the field of buying and selling using computer ordering the focus is on the transaction. We can compare this to buying and selling at the corner store, where the focus is on both the transaction and maintaining social relations.

- *Tenor*, which refers to interpersonal relations, that is, the relationship between speaker and hearer (or writer and reader) and any unintended audience. Thus, for example, we find that in electronic mail Italians use a more formal register than Americans and other English speakers, who use an informal, chatty style.
- *Mode*, which refers to both medium and the relation between language and what it is talking about. Thus, communication with or via a computer introduces a new medium of communication, one in which oral language is often presented in written form. Further, it presents a situation where the distance between participants or between the action and the participants is different from other types of communication.

That a particular text can be identified as bureaucratic register or a mystery novel depends not only on the characteristics of the text itself, but also on how it relates to all other texts – a concept often called intertextuality. My mystery novel is a mystery novel because it has characteristics of other mystery novels and because it does not have some of the features of a science fiction novel, or of a poem, or of a warranty agreement. As computers provide opportunities for novel ways of using language, we are left questioning how hybrid texts (such as hypertext) fit our current taxonomies of genres and registers.

Simplified register

One special type of register has been identified and is relevant to our discussion here – simplified registers, which result from particular aspects of the context in which the language is used. One type of simplified register results from the speaker's perception that the addressee (such as a baby, a non-native speaker, or a student) is incompetent in the language. Caretaker talk (e.g., Ferguson 1977), foreigner talk (e.g., Ellis 1985), and teacher talk (e.g., Henzl 1974; Gaies 1977) have been identified as such simplified registers. The goal of this simplification is to facilitate comprehension.

Simplification also may result from limitations in time or space, such as in telephones, newspaper headlines (e.g., Straumann 1935), advertising (e.g., Leech 1966), or note-taking (Janda 1985). Here, the goal is to provide efficient communication given limits in time or space.

We shall see throughout the following chapters that many interactions with and via computers involve simplified registers.

Functions of language

Whether written or spoken, language serves two basic functions: transactional and interactional. The transactional function is for the transfer of information, while the interactional function is for the maintenance of social relationships. Of course, many discourses involve both functions. However, as we examine language and computers, we will find that these two functions operate differently than in communication without computers, so, it is important to understand how they operate.

A service encounter at a supermarket meat counter may typically involve both functions. The customer asks for a pound of lean steak and the butcher negotiates with the customer as to which steak is the closest in weight and quality. Either during or after the encounter, customer and butcher may discuss the drought, or the high price of meat, or even their children. This latter communication has been called 'chat'. It does not move the encounter along; it does not provide essential information to the progress of the conversation; its goal is to establish empathy. Encounters that typically involve only chat are conversations between strangers or acquaintances at cocktail parties or on trains and planes. In these encounters, participants do not challenge each other or argue; they talk about mutually known information and change topic if one is not fruitful. Some transactional encounters are embedded in one type of chat, called phatic communication, which includes the greetings and farewells at the beginning and end of encounters such as a visit to the doctor or the ubiquitous 'You're welcome' at the end of a service encounter in the United States. How can we program computers to provide just the right amount of interactional discourse in a service encounter that is essentially transactional? The differences between transactional and interactional communication also occur in written language, although written language is more typically used primarily for information transfer, as in business letters, weekly magazines, brochures, etc. Written genres where interaction is primary include thank-you notes, postcards, and love letters.

We need to note here that, while all languages and cultures use language for both functions, the way these functions are realized in language varies. For example, in most English-speaking cultures, the customer says 'thank you' to the sales assistant. In many other cultures (e.g., Japan, China), customers never thank people who are performing the job for which they are paid. This is especially important when we consider transferring technology across cultural groups.

Cohesion, coherence and schemata

If we expect the promise of artificial intelligence to be fulfilled, computer programs will need to be able to interpret text and produce coherent texts. What exactly would such programs need to know to do this? As people interact with computers as they go about their lives, how do wordprocessing programs and style checkers affect the coherence of their texts? What expectations do we have of a computer interface, based on our knowledge and experience with human interaction?

Cohesion, coherence and schemata work together in any discourse, but I will discuss them separately before showing how they interact.

Cohesion refers to the linguistic ties used across sentences to indicate the connections between ideas in the discourse. The cohesive resources used by English are:

- reference (e.g., pronouns for nouns)
- substitution and ellipsis (e.g., 'that' for a phrase)
- conjunction (e.g, but, and, thus)
- lexical cohesion (e.g., collocation and words from a similar semantic field – baseball, bat, diamond).

The following short text illustrates a number of these devices (adapted from Yule 1985, p. 105):

> My father once bought a Lincoln convertible. He did it by saving every penny he could. That car would be worth a fortune nowadays.
> However, he sold it to help pay for my college education. I'd rather have the convertible, wouldn't you?

The pronouns 'he'/'he'; 'my'/'my'/'I'; 'it' are examples of reference that link together reference to the same outside reality (father, the writer, and the car). 'Wouldn't you?' is an example of ellipsis, where the intended meaning is 'Wouldn't you rather have the convertible?'.

'However' is a conjunction explicitly identifying the contrastive relationship between a car that could have been worth a fortune now, but was sold. Lexical cohesion is illustrated by the words related to cars – 'Lincoln', 'convertible', 'car' – and those related to money – 'bought', 'saving', 'penny', 'worth', 'fortune', and 'pay'.

Coherence for some researchers resides in the text; for others, it is a property of people. It is actually both at the same time, but primarily, it refers to the way people try to make sense of what they read and hear, regardless of the actual explicit cohesiveness of the text itself. The degree to which readers or listeners successfully grasp the intended meaning and relationships in the text depends largely on whether their expectations are consistent with the text. These expectations have been called schemata, that is, hierarchically structured mental representations of information that are founded on our previous experience with texts, with the world, and in particular with society and culture (see, for example, Kintsch 1988).

Speakers and writers can contribute to this interpretation by making their discourse coherent, that is, creating discourses in which individual propositions are related to each other in a culturally acceptable manner. Texts that meet reader expectations can be considered reader friendly. But, even when texts are not reader friendly, as in the non-native speaker example given earlier, we bring all our meaning-making abilities to bear on the text and make sense even out of apparent nonsense. Thus, for example, in the second sentence, 'The social rituals have been transferred from older generation to the other one', the referent for 'other one' is unclear. However, from our understanding of the world, we know that rituals are handed down from one generation to the next, so we have no trouble understanding the writer's intent. How does a style checker deal with such a text?

As we read or engage in spoken discourse, we draw from our previous knowledge, building and altering what are called schemata in the cognitive psychology literature. These schemata can be at many different levels of generality, from the structure of texts, to the structure of novels, to the structure of mystery novels, to the structure of Agatha Christie novels, to the structure of *Murder on the Nile*. The anticipatory schema we bring to a text helps us predict its structure – whether it is a scholarly text or a newspaper article – and thus what we can attend to – headings, abstracts, and so on. Thus, we find it easier to comprehend a text that follows the usual conventions for that genre.

Schemata are not static. They change constantly as we perceive new information. As we use the same information many times, its use becomes automatic. Take learning to drive a car as an example. When we first get behind the wheel, all the different pedals, levers, switches, and their operation are independent schemata. We think consciously 'How fast am I going? What gear am I in? Does the engine sound funny? Do I need to shift gears?'. We apply the rules as deliberate decision making. Once we become experts, we no longer apply the rules consciously. We recall whole schemata from the past and apply them without breaking them into their component parts. This is what some cognitive psychologists call intuition, which is not to be confused with guessing. Intuition is based on knowledge built up over time into whole schemata. This does not mean that, in certain situations (especially when things go wrong), experts do not still think analytically – but analytical thinking will follow the intuition that things are not proceeding normally. Can we expect artificial intelligence programs to reach such levels of expertise?

Schemata are built on background knowledge of various kinds, principally, textual knowledge, commonsense knowledge and cultural knowledge. Textual knowledge refers to intertextuality, discussed earlier. Commonsense knowledge refers to the knowledge that all humans have by virtue of living in the world – for example, that if I let go of the ball in my hand, it will fall to the ground. Cultural knowledge refers to the knowledge we acquire as members of a particular society, group, and so on. This knowledge includes the conventions of language use mentioned earlier in this chapter, or the interpretation of physical phenomena.

To illustrate the relationship among cohesion, coherence and schemata, let us look at the following two examples:

> Books are made of paper. Paper comes from trees. Trees grow in forests. Those forests are in Canada. Canada is a cold country. However, a cold is caused by germs.

> A: Have you got a light?
> B: Sorry, I don't smoke.

In the first example, we have a text that makes use of various cohesive devices (lexical cohesion, reference, conjunction); yet the text does not entirely make sense. In the second example, the only cohesive ties are the 'I'/'you' of dialogue and the lexical relationship between 'light' and 'smoke'; yet, we have no trouble interpreting the dialogue. The second text makes sense because of our previous experiences with the world and our knowledge that people do not ask 'Have you got a light?' as a yes/no question (see p. 22 below for more discussion on indirect speech acts). Thus, for discourse to make sense, it must be coherent according to our understanding of the world and, most writers and speakers indicate some of this coherence through the use of cohesive ties, thus making the discourse more reader or listener friendly.

This type of background knowledge that helps us interpret texts coherently can be very complex, as in the following restaurant schema (adapted from Schank and Abelson 1977):

> Jane went to a restaurant and had a hamburger and fries for lunch. She left a big tip.

If we come from the same culture, we will have similar schemata that help us interpret this text. We know Jane went through a door, sat at a table or counter, was waited on by a waitress or waiter and so on. We know it can not be McDonald's since we do not leave a tip at fast food restaurants. But, clearly, these schemata are not necessarily shared across different groupings of people. All of this knowledge needs to be coded into a computer program for artificial intelligence programs to interpret such texts as humans would.

Conversation

How do people organize talk in face-to-face and telephone conversations? What does this tell us about what we expect from computer interfaces and what computers would need to 'know' to be artificially intelligent? Most study of how conversations are organized has been conducted by ethnomethodologists, who are sociologists of language. They have proposed that conversation is a unit 'characterizable in terms of overall organization (such as openings and closings) in addition to the use of conversational activities like turn-taking' (Levinson, 1983, p. 318).

In face-to-face and telephone conversations, openings include self-identification, greetings, and summons with the hearer pairing these opening moves (e.g., Schegloff 1972; 1976). If a speaker says, 'Hi, how are you?' and we respond, 'Do you know where the milk is?' our contribution would be unexpected. However, there are, even in face-to-face and telephone conversations, situations where pairing is not the norm. This is especially the case if other means are used to provide the move. For example, in going up to a doctor's receptionist, I self-identify (unless I am a very familiar patient), but the receptionist does not, since her name is either marked on a sign on her desk, or is not considered relevant to the encounter. In telephone conversations, the ring of the telephone represents the summons. Closing elements have been identified as (Schegloff and Sacks 1973):

- closing implicative topic, e.g., making arrangements
- passing turn pairs (with pre-closings) e.g., 'okay'
- typing of the call e.g., 'thank you' as a response to a request that is fulfilled and
- terminal pairs e.g., 'bye'.

Again, as with opening moves, these are usually paired.

Turn-taking

Who speaks when is subject to socially defined rules. In casual conversation in mainstream Anglo culture, one party talks at a time (Sacks et al. 1974), achieved through the following principles:

- completion of a turn unit (e.g. sentence, clause, phrase) constitutes a potential transition to another speaker
- turn allocation operates because the current speaker can
  – select the next speaker or
  – let another speaker self-select or
  – continue.

The three choices listed are ordered as above and are recursive. In addition, there are turn-allocation techniques through which the current speaker gives the turn to another such as: tag questions (e.g., 'You like coffee, don't you?') as exit techniques; starting first; and sets of adjacency pairs, which consist of related, ordered pairs of utterances such as question/answer or an offer from an addressor followed by acceptance in the next turn by the addressee. Adjacency pairs require that the listener respond. Speakers can hold their turns by using fillers ('uhm', etc.) or cohesive conjunctions (and, but) that indicate to listeners that they are not finished, but intend to continue.

When people communicate via computers, how do they take turns? How do they open and close conversations? What are the conventions of this computer-mediated communication (CmC)? We will see that conventions have changed as computer-mediated communication has added another communication site to people's repertoire.

Speech acts

Speech act theory developed to explain what people use language for. As mentioned earlier, language serves two major functions – interaction and transactional. But, these two categories are too broad to provide adequate explanations of what speakers intend in actual discourse. Speech act theory then describes the acts speakers intend as follows (taken from Searle 1976):

1. *Representatives*: those acts that commit the speaker to the truth of the statement (e.g., asserting).
2. *Directives*: those acts through which the speaker attempts to get the listener to do something (e.g., requests, questions, commands).
3. *Commissives*: those acts that commit the speaker to some future action (e.g., promises, offers).
4. *Expressives*: those acts that express the speaker's psychological state (e.g., apologies, thanks).
5. *Declaratives*: those acts that effect a change by their very utterance (e.g., declaration of war, pronouncement of marriage, naming of a ship).

While this seems at first glance a neat, concise list of the functions of language, the difficulty lies in recognizing which utterances perform which speech acts. Not all statements are representatives; not all questions are only directives for information. If a friend comes into a room and you say 'You left the door open', the friend (and any other listener) would most likely interpret this not as an assertion about the door, but a request for the friend to close the door. While walking across campus, a student asks me 'Do you know where the Student Union is?' I could answer the question only (and literally), and say 'Yes'. But, that is not what the speaker intends – she wants me to tell her *where* the Student Union is. In other words, she was indirectly using a directive (a request). Examples such as these two are called indirect speech acts because their function can not be determined by the linguistic structure of the utterance. As functioning human beings, we can correctly interpret these speech acts only because of the context and our cultural knowledge. How can we design computer programs that allow for this subtlety of language? While indirect speech acts occur in all languages, their actual interpretation differs across cultures. In English, indirect speech acts such as 'Do you know ...? Would you mind ...? Could you ...?' are considered more polite and gentle than their direct counterparts (commands).

Conversation for action

Based on Flores' research in business and on the notion of speech acts, Winograd and Flores (1986) developed the notion of conversation for action, which I later developed further (Murray 1991). The basic idea is that, in the business environment, most conversations serve a transactional function and are requests by the speaker to get something done. The following network shows the basic structure of conversations for action:

(p. 106)

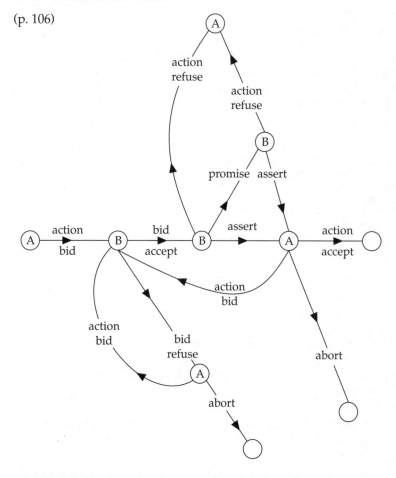

The main elements of conversation for action are the initial action bid (a request) and the responding action, which may or may not be accompanied by an assertion that the requested action has been completed. The person to whom the request is made (the requestee) can refuse the bid by renegotiating the conditions of the conversation, for example, the requestee may challenge the requestor's right to make the request. Once both agree on the conditions, the requestee accepts the bid by either promising (a commissive) to meet the request, refusing to meet it, or by carrying it out. We will see later how Flores used this model to develop a computer program to explicitly mould workplace conversations. Should speech acts be stated explicitly as he suggests? What function do indirect speech acts play?

The cooperative principle

Part of the reason why conversations work is that participants cooperate with each other, a principle developed by Grice (1975). He states this principle as 'Make your conversational contribution such as is required by the accepted purpose or direction of the talk exchange in which you are engaged.' In order to be cooperative, Grice claims, people follow four maxims:

1. *Quantity*: make your contribution as informative as is required, but not more, or less, than is required.
2. *Quality*: do not say that which you believe to be false or for which you lack evidence.
3. *Relation*: be relevant.
4. *Manner*: avoid ambiguity and obscurity, be clear, brief and orderly.

We apply these maxims in dialogues such as the one above ('Do you have a light?' 'Sorry, I don't smoke.'). The first speaker assumes the second speaker is being both relevant and informative, rather than merely making a comment about smoking. This answer contains an implicature, that is, additional meaning. To understand this additional meaning, we have to know that only smokers carry matches or lighters, that is, we need background knowledge.

In order to maintain the maxim of quantity and not give too much information, speakers make assumptions about what their hearers already know. These assumptions are called presuppositions.

If a speaker asks, 'Why did you arrive late?', she is assuming you did arrive late. Presuppositions are devices that lawyers and others make use of because it is difficult for the listener to respond without also making the same presupposition. Thus, lawyers ask 'Where did you buy the cocaine?' rather than 'Did you buy cocaine?'. The first example has a presupposition: that the person did in fact buy the cocaine and the only point in question is where.

How do we modify these conventions in communication using computers? When the computer program can not know what its user already knows, how can it be programmed not to be too brief or too verbose? When people communicate using computers, how do they co-operate? Do they change because they are using a written medium for what is essentially interactive conversation? We will see, for example, how novice users of bulletin boards do not know how to invoke these co-operative principles in a new medium.

Speech events

Speech events are culturally defined uses of language, such as debates, interviews and wedding ceremonies They are distinguished from other events, such as a day at the beach because language defines the event. A speech event may be a single sentence or speech act but usually consists of an internal structure with established features of content, linguistic form and use. In a speech event, many different registers may be used. For example, in a wedding ceremony, there is the register of the sermon, the register of the hymn, the register of the vows, etc. Speech events, then, may incorporate the rules of use already described – register, cohesion, coherence, speech acts, turn-taking and literacy. The interesting question for this book is how the characteristics of conventional speech events change when computers are introduced. For example, how is a sales transaction between computer and customer different from one between sales assistant and customer? How are bulletin-board conversations different from face-to-face conversations? The different medium results in a different configuration of language use, creating new speech events, with new conventions, many of which are still evolving since the medium is still new.

LITERACY AND ORALITY

An understanding of literacy is important because 1) many analysts of information technologies note the striking similarity between the introduction of alphabetic writing in Ancient Greece, the advent of the printing press in fifteenth-century Europe and the introduction of computer technology in the late twentieth century, and 2) popular belief is that current (and future) information technologies are reducing the need for literacy, that we are in a literacy 'crisis'. Thus, I will discuss both of these claims in this chapter and then in later chapters I will show how the introduction of information technology forces us to rethink the nature of the social construct we call literacy.

The supposed literacy crisis has been attributed to our children's concentration on television, video games and computers, to the exclusion of printed books. Greene (1983, p. 6C) eschews electronic mail, preferring typewritten or handwritten letters because, as he says:

> All the personality and humanity that show up in letters disappear on computer screens . . . all the warmth and wisdom are translated into those frigid, uniform, green characters.

Walter Ong (1977; 1982), a scholar who has written widely on orality, literacy and technology, goes even further when he claims that

> Writing is passive, out of it, in an unreal, unnatural world. So are computers.

> (Ong 1982, p. 79)

Both writers express concern at how new media can express human thought. By including writing, Ong echoes Plato, who has Socrates point out that writing might weaken memory and writers might have the show of wisdom without the reality. With the later advent of print, scholars and other power brokers feared the destruction of memory, that print would weaken the mind or spirit. Pope Alexander VI, for example, declared (quoted in McCorduck 1985, p. 23)

> It will be necessary to maintain full control over the printers so that they may be prevented from bringing into print writings which are antagonistic to the Catholic faith or which are likely to cause trouble to believers.

From his perspective, he was right to fear the printed word; printed books were cheap and widely available, so widely available that a local quarrel in Germany was transformed into the Reformation.

It is easy to dismiss comments such as those by Plato, Pope Alexander, Ong or Greene as reactionary, Luddite responses by those who want to maintain the status quo and fear loss of power or prestige. These fears are probably justified: just as the advent of writing altered the status of the epic poets as transmitters of information and the invention of printing changed the status of the scholar-priests in the middle ages, so too might the computer result in new institutions that will replace the University, radio, television, and newspapers as knowledge brokers. While this is an important sociopolitical issue, I believe even more important issues emerge: How do different technologies affect the uses of language? How did the introduction of a written alphabet, the printing press and the computer, impact upon our ways of thinking? Was Marshall McLuhan right when he claimed that 'the medium is the message', that each medium of communication produces particular social relations and a particular form of consciousness? As we move from the era of print to that of computers, what does it mean socially and cognitively to be literate?

To place the advent of information technology in its historical perspective, I will begin by tracing the development of literacy and, more importantly, the development of scholarship about literacy, its nature and its consequences.

According to Havelock (1982), the development of the alphabet in Ancient Greece resulted in new ways of thinking, new ways of looking at the world, and new ways of describing it. The advent of the printing press is also thought to change human cognition. According to Eisenstein (1979), by mechanizing human memory, the printing press made food for thought more abundant, allowing mental energies to be much more efficiently used. Print provided us with fixed forms of reference, ways of organizing our intellectual life, categorizing, indexing and making permanent. For researchers such as Goody and Watt (1968), literacy reshapes consciousness: the kinds of analysis involved in the syllogism and in other forms of logical procedure are clearly dependent upon writing.

> Like written language, mechanical printing acted as an artificial
> memory, but now the memory, a communal treasure, was greatly
> enlarged. Such growth illustrates what scientists like to call 'the order of
> magnitude effect', the idea that if something is increased by tens, by

hundreds, by thousands, and by millions, there will come about not only a quantitative change but a qualitative change as well.

(McCorduck 1985, p. 34)

Each change (from oral language to written, from ideographic writing to alphabetic writing, from hand writing to printed text) is seen as an advance in human cognition.

Thus, these scholars view oral and written language as dichotomous: writing is the suitable vehicle for rational, critical thinking; writing is analytic and sequential; meaning and authority are lodged 'in the text'; oral language is personal and emotional; oral language is formulaic; spoken discourse is context-bound. Recent researchers such as Tannen (1982) and Halliday (1985) suggest instead an oral/literate continuum with academic writing and casual conversations representing two maximally differentiated styles on the oral-literate continuum. Such research has identified strategies associated with orality, and others associated with literacy: strategies such as integration and lack of personal involvement are associated with writing while strategies such as fragmentation and personal involvement are associated with speaking. However, most of these researchers begin by assuming that a stretch of discourse is either written or oral, rather than by considering different discourse samples as part of the linguistic repertoire of the speech community, which is the view of scholars who see literacy as socioculturally constructed, a 'way of taking meaning from the environment' (Heath 1983, p. 49).

These scholars such as Heath (1983), Pattison (1982) and Street (1984) have shown that certain types of consciousness may be antecedent to literacy, rather than its consequence. Just as writing was the vehicle for changes in Greek culture and thought, the printing press facilitated changes already beginning to take place in Europe, especially a heightened sense of individuality and personality, of nationalism and secularism.

If literacy is socially constructed, what does this mean for our supposed 'literacy crisis'? Holzman (1989) discusses two types of literacy – 'nominal' and 'active' and says that very few in the developed world are actually illiterate, lacking alphabetic literacy; but large numbers are nominally literate, that is, they have gone to school, they can read and write (usually to fifth grade level) but hardly ever use those skills. He says both the Roadville and Trackton folk described by Heath are nominally literate. This is a much more attractive name than functionally literate since the latter implies they can function and in fact do not need any more. The Trackton and Roadville children's ways with words described by Heath did not help them with the ways with words of the schools. So, if we view literacy as a social practice, we see that some literacy practices are not consonant with those of the school or academic literacy. 'We should not view the literacy crisis or the literacy practices and failures of our students to be failures to grapple with the *technologies* of reading and writing. They are failures of participation in and identification with a particular sociocultural group' (Murray 1990, p. 610).

> In a political-economic system increasingly based on information (for communication, command, and control), there are frightening consequences of this fundamental transformation in the labor market for those whose literacy skills are mainly nominal. The small percentage of the population who are truly illiterate, and this very large number whose literacy skills are only nominal, face increasingly bleak futures economically, socially, culturally. People who do not actively use literacy in their everyday lives are likely to contribute little to decision making, to the setting of social, political, or business goals, likely to remain dominated by those who do.
>
> (Holzman 1989, p. 166)

In many ways, the computer and the printing press appear to be parallel phenomena: both are intellectual technologies, processors of information, products of evolving technology, and both were resisted by the establishment. However there are major differences both in the scope of their technology and the effects each has on language and intellectual life. One such difference lies in the way the technology acts as a device for receiving, storing and transmitting human language. Whether they are similar or not, we will find that, as with the advent of the alphabet and the printing press, we can not make the claim that changes in consciousness and language are necessarily a *result* of information technology. The relationship among language, social life and technology is organic.

In this chapter, I have briefly sketched some of the ways humans use language as they go about their daily lives. I have focused only on those aspects of language and communication that are pertinent to our discussion of language and information technology. The remaining chapters will discuss various applications of information technology and how they impact or are impacted by human communication systems, drawing on the background information in this chapter.

THREE

The computer at work

It is in the workplace that people first come in contact with explicit computer technology. Their livelihood so often depends on how they adapt to the technology; rarely is the technology adapted to them. According to Brod (1984), information technology operates in two zones – the private, for conducting our personal lives (e.g., banking, mail ordering) and the production, 'where we depend on computers to perform our work. Both zones affect us, but since computers are more likely to be a constant presence in the production zone, it is here we find ourselves influenced by computers most drastically' (p. 27). Most demand for the new technologies has come from industry, the state and the military. Consumer demand for personal, cultural and informational services is quite limited.

We have all heard or read about the possible effects of video display terminals on health and of repetitive typing on muscles and of surveillance of workers via computers. But, the media have not paid as much attention to the effects of computers in the workplace on communication among people and between the computer and the worker. Robert Howard, author of *Brave New Workplace*, claims that the introduction of information technologies into the workplace has resulted in an increased distance between workers and top management, a more fragile system, and destruction of the social systems that support existing work environments. These three factors all contribute to changes in the use of language since human language is not only context-embedded, that is, determined by the context, but also a power for altering the context. While not denying the importance of both psychological and physiological factors, this chapter will focus on the way computers in the workplace affect human–machine and human–human communication.

THE COMPUTER INTERFACE

Most people have experienced the blank screen of a computer, a screen that gives no indication of what the user should do. Donald Norman (1988), who has studied human interaction with machines in general, says that the computer is especially vulnerable to poor design because its abstract nature amplifies all the usual problems found in the design of technology. Most users have no understanding of the internal workings of either the hardware or software–nor do they want it. It is not only the blank screen that is perplexing. Even with a manual, system commands are not intuitive. In early machines, users had to learn arcane key combinations to get the computer to do what they wanted. This is still true of many systems in operation in the workplace, such as the airlines reservation systems used by travel agents in the United States. Interestingly, many of the early terms for interacting with the computer drew on military metaphors, perhaps largely because the military funded much of the computer research and was the largest purchaser of computer systems in the United States. Thus, we have terms such as 'command', 'abort', 'escape', 'crash', and 'kill the program'.

> A well-known computer company decided to redesign its computer keyboard. To test the design, they had many people use the keyboard, adapting it until it was user friendly. When the keyboard became a product and was used by customers and internally within the company, users complained bitterly about the complex key combinations they had to use to perform even the most basic commands, such as clear screen, move to bottom of the screen, etc. The company had used data entry clerks to test the keyboard. Thus, the keyboard was designed to have single keystrokes for their tasks, not for wordprocessing or programming, the functions used by most users.

Xerox was the first company to try to implement a more effective system, one with easy-to-use commands and 'obvious' visual displays. Xerox's hardware, however, could not keep up with the software, resulting in unacceptable time lags between asking the computer to perform a function and its actual performance. It was Apple Computer that took many of these basic breakthroughs (e.g., the mouse, visual displays), tried it on the unsuccessful Lisa and then on the Macintosh, leading to the window and pull-down menu interface so familiar today. Certainly these approaches were a breakthrough from a blank screen or a non-intuitive command sequence such as Ctrl-Alt-Del to reboot the system. However, despite advertisements to the contrary, the interface is not necessarily natural and intuitive. Who has not tried to perform some simple wordprocessing function, only to find it impossible to work out how to do it without both a manual *and* knowledge of the name of the function. Who would automatically look up 'hanging indent' when wanting to have the first line flush with the margin and the second indented (especially used in typing references)? Or that using the shift key allows the user to move *only* the top flag in the ruler (used to produce a hanging indent)? Nor are icons self-evident. Take the piece of paper with the top right-hand-corner turned down ⃞. This is now the default industry standard for 'open new document'. Is this an obvious icon? Or, one I was recently introduced to–a globe on a stand ⊕ . When asked what it stood for, I suggested 'different languages', (i.e., I expected that you could point to that icon to make menu choices of what language you wanted to write your document in). I did not guess right. It stands for networking. Currently, the two primary modes for choosing a function on a computer are keyboard commands or pointing to an icon. The first is limited by the number of keys on the keyboard; the second by the number of universal, intuitively understood icons. The former is rather like learning a new language, with different combinations of symbols representing different concepts. However, unlike language, there are no 'rules' for how these symbols are combined. Their combination is based on some individual's view of the world. The latter is like the early use of pictographic writing, where, for example, a man might be represented by the 'picture': ⵌ The limitations of one-to-one symbolic representation led to the development of ideographic writing, syllabic writing systems, or alphabets. These systems allow us to represent abstractions and function words in a language.

Even more importantly, we have exchanged the military metaphor for one of a desktop. For those of us familiar with office work, the desktop is a robust metaphor, with its file folders, telephones, rolodexes, and cut and paste. However, if the computer is to be the universal machine, the metaphor must be accessible to all, not just office workers. The current visual metaphors privilege one class and group of people only. Do we wonder then that users make errors as they try to 'read' the interface?

AIRLINE RESERVATIONS AUTOMATED

A grandmother, wanting to fly out to visit her son and his family for a couple of weeks' vacation calls Alligator Airlines and asks the fare for flights from San Francisco to New York. The first question the reservation agent asks is 'When are you travelling?' Since the grandmother is looking for the cheapest fare and date of travel is irrelevant, she just nominates a month – 'Oh, probably May'. The reservation agent then asks, 'What date in May?' Again, the grandmother doesn't care; she wants the cheapest fare. So, the agent checks mid-week fares and finds that if she leaves mid-week and returns mid-week, the fare is cheaper. So, the agent selects a mid-week date in May (the 16th) and tells the grandmother, 'There are two non-stop flights that day, 10:00am and 6:00pm. Which would you prefer?' The grandmother asks what time each arrives, and decides that the 10:00am is more convenient. So, the agent then says, 'OK, then, I'll book you on the 10:00am flight on May 16th. What's your name? Now, for your return. How long do you want to stay?' By now, the grandmother is confused since she never had a particular date in mind. So, she tells the agent she'll have to check dates with her son and call back.

This scenario illustrates the implementation of computer monitoring on the discourse style and conversational moves of these airline employees. In her book, *The Electronic Sweatshop*, Barbara Garson (1988) details the effect of computerization on the working lives of many different types of workers – from McDonald's clerks to a Wall Street broker. The case of Alligator (aka American) Airlines illustrates how communication gets redefined when efficiency experts apply the rules for streamlining manufacturing to service industries. Time-and-motion studies applied to manufacturing in the nineteenth century are now being applied to office work; only now they are aided by the computer as the monitoring device par excellence. The notion behind time-and-motion studies is that if a particular job can be broken down into all its component tasks and each task is measured and its most efficient performance is determined, then the job can be rationalized and hence, made more efficient. The workers first get new tools to improve the speed of their routine tasks and then, since the next step is to automate these tasks, they have machines perform them instead of people. Leaving aside issues of quality and of human alienation, such rationalization usually did produce more products in manufacturing industries – more cars, more cans, more computer chips – at lower prices. Just as the industrial revolution extended human physical capabilities, the information revolution will extend human mental capabilities, it is believed. But, when applied to service (and other) industries where human communication is the core of the job, the very nature of the job changes.

American Airlines decided to rationalize their reservation agents' jobs. First they identified two general types of calls: action and potential. An action call is where the customer knows where and when she is travelling and asks for reservations. A potential call is from someone like the grandmother in the scenario above. The sign of a good reservation agent is that he can convert the potential call into an action call.

To determine how this could be achieved most efficiently, American then broke down the conversations between agent and customer into modules. Each speech act of the agent was identified – acts such as opening, probe, sales pitch, close, address; each speech act of the customer was identified – acts such as resist. Agents were trained to use certain types of presupposition questions rather than yes/no questions in the probe. Thus, in the scenario above, the agent asks the grandmother 'Which would you prefer, the 10:00am or the 6:00pm?' Here, the presupposition is that the listener wants one of these. A yes/no question such as 'Do you want to book?' on the other hand has no such presupposition. They were trained to try to close, that is, ask for the person's name so they can start the booking process. In addition to standardizing the conversations between reservation agents and customers, American uses the computers to monitor these conversations. Supervisors on-site and at company headquarters listen in to conversations and report on whether the agent probed or used the caller's name. The computer also tracks the talk time, the amount of time the agent is actually plugged in, the time spent making the reservation online after the end of the phone call, and the conversions (the enquiries 'converted' into bookings). Pay rises depend on these statistics. However, American found that their customers complained that the reservation agents were too aggressive and many of the conversions never actually boarded the plane – presumably people made the reservation just to get off the phone! Thus, American has instituted a new rating system where the subjective qualities (such as politeness or consideration of the customer) of the conversation are used, as well as the talk time and boarding, rather than conversion. However, the standardized conversation is still in place – it is only that one aspect of monitoring that has changed.

American Airlines is a case study of the belief in perfect technical control of the workplace, with its monitoring and emphasis on quantity over quality. But, what has happened to the conversation of our grandmother? Her wishes and language have been manipulated to get a sale. Thus, she ends with three alternatives: hang up and try again, take the reservation being offered by the agent, or visit a travel agent who will access the same computer as the reservation agent, but who will discuss different schedules, different fares, etc. While airlines have attempted to standardize telephone call conversations, no-one has standardized face-to-face conversation in such encounters. Another alternative exists – online reservations from home. Through one such computer service, I am able to check airline schedules, fares, food, aircraft, and so on, online. I can even make the reservation online or I can use this information to call the airlines as an action call.

But, for those of us who must interact with pre-programmed clerks, the interaction is at best efficient, at worst a disaster. Since the clerks are pre-programmed, they do not listen to any hidden meanings (implicatures) in our conversation – they are only cuing on the key words of place, time, etc. This is a virtual conversation and perhaps will be better when it is automated, for then customers will not expect real communication from real people; but, that would lead to loss of jobs.

What has happened to the interaction reservation agents had with each other? Now, every keystroke is counted; every break is noted. Since work occupies most of our waking time, for most people it is more than a place to work – it is a place to make friends, to socialize, to discuss ideas about the job and about life in general. As Brod (1984, p. 49) notes: 'informal chatting at work helps us stay in touch with what others are doing, view our own work from a broader perspective, gather second opinions on particular work-related problems, and recuperate from prolonged periods of focused work'. Many times, informal chatting about work or non-work can result in serendipitous leads to new ideas and new ways of seeing our work. To stay creative, we need to explore ideas with others and within ourselves. Automated knowledge workers in fact have less opportunity to explore ideas within themselves than do automated assembly line workers. Assembly line workers' minds are free to think, explore, and create while they perform repetitious manual tasks. Knowledge workers, even when performing routinized tasks, are using their minds.

The issue illustrated by this example is that the airline has used models of human–human communication inappropriately, as well as inappropriately applying procedures that worked for different technology.

1. The airline in our example did study their reservation agents' conversations to determine openings, closings, turn-taking, speech acts and so on; however, they then collapsed all the possible permutations these conversations may take into one standardized model. Apart from phatic communication (which represents a small part of human conversations), we do not use prefabricated conversations.
2. Further, conversation fulfills two functions: transaction and interaction. By focusing on transaction, the airline removed any opportunity for interaction from the conversations between their reservation agents and customers or between reservation agents.
3. As a model for computerization, the airline used the time-and-motion study model of manufacturing. When dealing with time-and-mind situations, the whole is more than the sum of its parts. Thus, breaking down conversations into their component parts and putting them back together does not make for a user-friendly service encounter.

SPORTSWRITING AUTOMATED

Read each of the following introductions to published stories about the same basketball game. Two were written by human sportswriters, one by a computer program. Which is which?

STORY NO. 1:
Golden State's Latrell Sprewell scored 26 points and had two key steals in the last two minutes as the Warriors rallied to beat San Antonio Spurs 106–101 Tuesday at San Antonio.

The warriors had led by 22 with 5:22 left in the second quarter in a win carried by a strong first quarter.

STORY NO. 2:
In a game that featured a blown 22-point lead, six technicals, two ejections and one rain delay, the Golden State Warriors stole a 106–101 victory over the San Antonio Spurs last night at the Alamodome.

This kind of win, said Assistant Coach Gregg Povovoch, who took over when Don Nelson was ejected, does not happen all the time.

STORY NO. 3:
Hail fell, the roof leaked, the Warriors swooned, Chris Webber arrived, Byson Houston left, Coach Don Nelson followed and the Warriors somehow recovered.

Or, to put it more simply, so many dramatic events took place in the Alamodome on Tuesday night that Dennis Rodman almost looked ordinary.

(Ochwat 1994, pp. 1F, 6F, 7F)

Yes, the first story was written by a computer. Did you guess based on your own schemata and knowledge of how baseball stories are written? Did you expect to have the coaches mentioned? To have quotations from players or coaches? If I had given further text, you would have found quotations from coaches. In fact, the first story works and is read in isolation as a 'real', not a 'virtual' sports story *because* the programmer has analysed the essential content features of a sports story: key events, quotations, team statistics, names of players and coaches. The coach of a team completes a questionnaire that asks for this information, which can then be plugged into the program, which constructs the news story. The text produced by the program does need some editing, but it can be done by a reporter with no knowledge in sports. If the coach does not write complete sentences or uses abbreviations, a human has to intervene. The program, *Sportswriter* was written by a sportswriter and so the shell into which the data are plugged fits the style of sports stories: short, punchy sentences, past tense, direct speech, action verbs. Most readers of stories it produces are not aware the story is the result of a program.

What trips the program up is unexpected events like the rain and hail that happened during half-time and caused the second-half to be delayed. To accommodate this, the program 'wrote', 'In the final half, the game was delayed for 12 minutes. . .' (p. 6F). The program is used extensively for high school sports, allowing many events and schools to be covered by small, poor, local newspapers. However, even the writer of the program is refusing to market it, for fear it will erode jobs. Like all other forms of automation, it could result in workers using lower level functions. But, like the translation programs discussed in Chapter 7, a human still has to do the final editing and editing is a higher level skill.

This is not artificial intelligence or an expert system. The program works primarily through pattern-matching, by inserting the particular information into slots in a pre-written script.

In addition to the question of jobs, this example also raises the issue of what is a text? Clearly the product is a text. A slot-filler works in this case because sports stories follow a formulaic script. We could all do similar things with fairy tales. In fact, this principle is often used to help novice writers. They are asked to take a well-written text and write their own story/narrative/description, etc., following the style of the original. Many of the texts we produce and read each day are more formulaic than creative – filling out forms, letters of complaint, and so forth. In fact, there is even a class of text called 'form letter' into which a clerk or secretary can plug variable data. The program merely semi-automatizes one type of such text. To become a sportswriter for a major newspaper also takes creativity, background knowledge of the teams and the sport, and of all the possibilities for writing a sports story.

PEDAGOGY AUTOMATED?

A gifted teacher of history stands in a classroom in California and teaches her 12th grade class about the American Civil War. The lesson is videotaped and beamed to 100 other schools across the nation. Students at the 100 sites have a teacher's aide, video cameras, computers, and telephones. The technology allows the students to 'talk'with the teacher – by telephone or by computer. The video cameras allow the teacher to 'see' the students at any site as she chooses. Once the lesson is over, the teacher's aide helps the students at their site with questions and to study for the upcoming test. The teacher's aide can use computer programs on the Civil War for students to use. With a CD ROM, students can see pictures and movies about the period.

This scenario is not possible now for schools, but has been trialled in high-tech companies to deliver their own training. It could be possible if the Information Superhighway has all the necessary features. Distance learning of this sort is expected to make learning more equitable – children from the poorest areas could have access to the best teachers. However, this scenario makes some fundamental assumptions both about learning and the role of teachers. It assumes that students learn by having material presented to them. However, research shows that teachers are most successful and most learning takes place when teachers tap into the knowledge and schemata children bring with them to the class-room (Bell and Stern, 1994). For example, students coming from Cambodia or Lebanon already have experienced civil war. When teachers start with that knowledge, the time-remote American Civil War becomes a reality for these students. 'Learning occurs when students actively build upon their own knowledge and coopera-tively interact with peers and teachers' (p. 4). Such distance learning projects are often promoted to decrease costs. However, if they are to be implemented in pedagogically sound ways, they are very expensive, requiring not only technology, but also teachers skilled at using it and incorporating it effectively in their own sylla-bus. Current estimates are that a good education program for one class period takes approximately 100 to 600 production hours (Woodbury 1994).

This scenario also illustrates the role of teachers. The gifted teacher in this case, is seen merely as the deliverer of information. The aides, who would in fact be providing the most instruction, are limited by the technology. They (and current teachers) do not have the time to spend on curriculum development to incorporate technology meaningfully into their lessons. So, pressed for time, they accept pre-packaged software, frequently written by pro-grammers rather than educators, often following a banking model of education rather than an inquiry-based one. Teachers become unskilled aides, implementing someone else's educational plan for their children. Only one or two teachers per school are likely to have the technical skills to write the programs (even with pro-gramming help) and maintain the equipment. So, although millions of computers are in schools, many are used for drill-and-practice, as a treat for 'good' students, or are largely ignored. In fact, Apple has found that the market has all but dried up – largely because teachers do not know what to do with the computers. Apple has begun working with professional associations to pro-duce videos of best practices. The experts from the professional organizations help choose what clips are sound pedagogically. In one such video (*Making Connections*), supported by NABE (National Association of Bilingual Education) and TESOL (Teachers of English to Speakers of Other Languages), a New York teacher has students with very limited English use the computer to design a house, complete with the dimensions. She then has them build the house from cardboard. It works – not so much because of the computer, although that is certainly an aid, but because the teacher herself 'expects a lot from her students'. She is there, constantly helping them, demanding their best despite their limited English.

Technology can be useful in education, but education should not be designed around the technology. Rather, the technology should be chosen because it fits the curriculum and fits the way students learn. Teachers should be left to do what they do best – teach, not become computer programmers or conduits for other's plans. We need to use the research we have on the interactions between learners and teachers in classrooms to incorporate technology in ways that optimize learning potential; to understand 'that if you control the computer it's a tool, if it controls you it's a weapon' (Garson 1988, p.245).

ELECTRONIC MAIL IN THE WORKPLACE

With more and more office workers working at computer terminals, electronic mail (e-mail) has begun to replace the water cooler or coffee machine as the hub for chatting. Within IBM more than 200,000 employees use VNET (the electronic mail system). William H. Gates, Chairman of Microsoft Corporation, runs his company largely through e-mail, used by most of the 5,000 employees. Decisions about products, vacation policy and so on are discussed, debated, and announced online. Gates himself receives and sends hundreds of e-mail notes a day, from employees at all levels and from all sectors of the company. Wendy's International (the fast food chain) has replaced mail couriers with e-mail, using it for marketing, sales, payroll, pricing, and even to edit field officers' speeches. These systems were designed and implemented to facilitate work; but they are also used for chat.

> Johnson [Wendy's supervisor of client support services] says, 'If they phone instead of using e-mail, it takes twice as long, because they chit-chat.' E-mail has dampened this tendency – but not completely. As Johnson notes, the Michigan office has been known to send 'We beat Ohio State!' greetings to the Ohio office.
>
> (First 1988, p. 212)

These computer networks become speech communities, linking people hundreds or thousands of miles apart. Lines of communication are restructured, as in the example of Microsoft, where Gates talks with any employee via e-mail.

Control

However, the question of control becomes crucial. Although companies tell employees not to use telephones for personal communication, they can not enforce this rule easily, especially in the United States, where telephone surveillance is illegal. So, the use of e-mail becomes attractive. As Johnson indicates, chitchat is reduced. But, even more importantly, e-mail surveillance is both easy and legal. This control raises the important issue of what language and information are public and what private. This issue of the control of electronic networks will be raised again in detail in Chapter 8. But, here, let me give an example of software designed to help control workplace communications, one that illustrates the tension between the employee wanting more efficiency in electronic communication and wanting to choose when she says what to whom and how.

The Coordinator: an example of control

Let us examine one application, a computer system called The Coordinator that supports interactive work in organizations (especially by managers, whose major function is to get work done through discourse). For Flores and his colleagues (1988, p. 171), 'Good design is an ontologically grounded intervention that allows work to flow smoothly with a minimum of breakdowns'. Based on this view of design, and on the Winograd and Flores model of conversation for action, the system requires that the sender define what type of communication the e-mail is – request, decline, promise, and so on. If the sender makes a request, the system prompts for a 'respond-by' date, a 'complete-by' date, and an 'alert' date. The system keeps track of the conversation so that at any time, one of the participants can check what requests they have asked that have not been fulfilled, or what promises they have made that they have not yet been fulfilled. In some ways, this system is a development of the inter-office memo slip that had 'Action', 'FYI', 'Route' and so on to signify what the sender intended the recipient to do with the information. While the program is based on sound design principles and an adequate theory of the way discourse works in an office environment, does it truly 'allow work to flow more smoothly'? Many users have found it actually hampers their communication work.

The system also includes a 'free-form' e-mail, where the sender does not have to identify what type of communication she is carrying out. Of course, as with all linguistic choices, the choice of free-form signals that the message is *not* a request! In initial implementations of the system, many people overwhelmingly used free-form since they did not want to go through the rigmarole of making choices or felt constrained by doing so. In Flores' interpretation of conversation for action, information does not exist – most workplace conversation is for the purpose of getting something done. In the business world, memos, and so on with 'FYI' attached are useless since the recipient does not know what he should do with the information (often a photocopy of an article) and so often either files it (without reading it) or throws it away. In more recent implementations, The Coordinator, while still including free-form, also includes 'Conversation for Possibilities'. This recognizes the serendipitous nature of conversation I alluded to earlier. Often, our initial e-mail may be 'for your information'. But, the information may lead to some conversation for action with requests and so on at a later date. So, what are the problems associated with this application?

1. Although based on both a study of conversation in the workplace, and on a principled theory of language use, Flores' system has not gained wide acceptance and has met with initial hostility from many users. The issue here is not whether the model is appropriate (it clearly is) but whether explicitly identifying speech acts is appropriate. For Flores, it is appropriate because it unveils hidden agendas; it makes explicit what is already there. It clarifies interaction because it is presumed that everyone knows what everyone else really means by what they say. Yet, it is ambiguity that so often leads to new possibilities, as well as to miscommunications.

2. Online conversations, like face-to-face conversations, are embedded within other conversations; utterances often carry more than one speech act or instances of a speech act (e.g., a request); several requests (or promises, etc.) are made in one e-mail message. The Coordinator does not accommodate this type of conversation very easily. Thus, I could not promise to send a colleague a

paper she has requested and in the same e-mail ask her to write me a letter of recommendation – these would be parts of two different conversations in the Winograd and Flores model and therefore must take two different message types. Given the choice of having to make a different menu choice in order to do this, most users would choose not to bother.

To use The Coordinator, users face restrictions on what they can say when and how; but they also gain the ability to track their conversations, overcoming a major drawback of most e-mail systems (recall my husband's 95 messages waiting for him after a few days out of town – how can he keep track of all these conversations?). Thus, the issue here is how much restriction and change are worth the pay off in enhanced organization of e-mail?

3. Winograd and Flores themselves argue that there is no objective world that can be measured; the world is created through the language we use to communicate. They believe that making the actions in conversation transparent to the participants helps focus the commitment to action required for business interaction. However, The Coordinator also falls into the trap of hiding its biases through language. By objectifying the speech acts in conversations for action (which is a verifiable model of work interactions), it hides the other types of interactions that take place in the work environment. Although workers may be exhorted not to gossip in company time, much gossip can become the basis for innovative, creative new work. Flores and his colleagues claim that these non-conversations for action should perhaps take place in face-to-face conversations around the coffee pot or in chance encounters, or, in the future 'there will be a mix in which computer-based text is used for the more explicit forms, while recorded and transmitted voice and video images become the preferred mode for less structured types of conversation that must occur at a distance' (1988, p. 167). To restrict media in this way seems counter to the natural way humans interact. As Flores admits, The Coordinator (and any other technology) is a form of intervention – the question will always be to what extent does the intervention facilitate human–human interaction and to what extent does it interfere?

AUTOMATING THE OFFICE

Office work was the first information domain to be automated, especially with the introduction of word processors. Companies use one of three basic strategies for implementing the new technology – centralization, autonomy, and work council. The first two are by far the most prevalent, especially in the United States. Centralization involves central planning, central control, with the system distributed down through the hierarchy. In addition to producing worker alienation, this type of implementation results in individual departments not having the system adapted to their specific needs. Autonomy (this is most prevalent in universities) occurs where individual departments are left free to introduce their own automation systems.

While this provides flexibility, it results in lack of compatibility and inefficiency. One department can not talk to another through a network; files can not be transferred; expertise and experience with a system can not be shared. The third implementation through work councils (done primarily in Europe) is what is often called participatory design, which emphasizes extensive prototyping and user involvement in the entire design and development process. Participatory design began because unions, seeing the possibility of lay-offs resulting from computerization, demanded that they be part of the introduction of any new technology. Thus, workers, managers, and systems analysts all contribute to the design and testing of any new systems. As a result, workers feel committed to the new technology and the design is one that enhances their job, not diminishes it. In participatory design, the introduction of systems is only considered successful if users accept the system, it fulfills their requirements, in addition to it being more efficient. The difficulty with participatory design is that it requires that workers have the technical knowledge to make appropriate decisions, and that they want to participate.

In a detailed study of *Managing Organizational Innovation: The Evolution from Word Processing to Office Information Systems,* Johnson and Rice (1987) use the effects of the introduction of wordprocessing as indicative of the effects of other information systems. After examining nearly 200 organizations, they developed the following principles:

1. Involve members in changing the technology and social system jointly to accomplish organizational mission.

2. Provide experiences for continuous learning.
3. Encourage experimentation; systems evolve, and managers must continuously attend to adaptation.
4. Design work units to promote communication.
5. Promote self-regulation of work groups through autonomy; locate the decision making at the task requiring the decision.
6. Design jobs so that people can perceive and complete a whole task.
7. Administer policies with flexibility.
8. Design jobs for upward mobility.
9. Establish boundaries so that recognizable success can lead to claims of expertise and authority.
10. Attend to the environment outside the boundaries.

It is clear from these recommendations that centralized introduction of new technologies is unlikely to provide such an environment since workers would not be involved in decisions about initial implementation or ongoing adaptation; nor is an autonomous system since it does not have permeable boundaries – a worker is unlikely to be able to move to another department since he would probably have to learn a new system. Like participatory design, this model calls for an increase in the communication between knowledge worker, manager and systems experts. Isolating workers with small tasks is bound to fail. Thus, discourse and interaction are essential to the successful introduction of information systems into the office.

'REAL EXECUTIVES DON'T USE COMPUTERS'

This title, playing on the anti-yuppie statement 'Real men don't eat quiche', was the headline for a 1984 newspaper article by Robert Hollis in *The San José Mercury News*. For the article he interviewed many chief executive officers (CEOs) and other executives in major Silicon Valley companies, finding that they either did not even have a computer or terminal on their desks or seldom used them. As one cynical observer at United Technologies put it: 'What these guys are saying is, "Do as I say, not as I do".' Some executives excused their lack of use by claiming they spend most of their time in meetings, travelling, or on the phone. Others said they could not remember passwords, could only type one finger at a time, and had secretaries. Yet, there are exceptions, such as Bill Gates, whom I mentioned earlier. In my own observations (and Brod 1984 also notes this), I have noted that many top level executives consider typing a secretarial function and do not wish to be seen doing it. Others, like the general public and their own workers, are frightened they will make mistakes and be shown to be incompetent.

Face-saving

A perhaps apocryphal tale runs like this. Before the advent of personal computers, individual workers had terminals in their offices that were linked directly to the large mainframe computers in a large, air-conditioned computer room. A certain mystique grew around these computer rooms – the computer operators and programmers were the only ones who knew and understood the technology. In this particular large computer company, upper level management never used the terminals in their offices. Instead, they relied on secretaries to type their memos, access information and so on. Despite all attempts to get these managers to use the new technology, they resisted – and no one knew why. After all, these were intelligent people *and* in a company that made its living selling computers!

Then came the personal computer. Each manager had a computer in his or her office. The computer could work as a stand-alone machine, but could also be tied into the mainframe computer and networks. Suddenly, typing could be heard coming from behind the closed office doors. In a relatively short time, these former Luddites (or at least that is what the 'techies' thought they were) began using electronic mail, typing their own documents, filling out forms online and so on. They did so largely because they were able to learn how to use the computer in a completely face-saving environment. Previously, when everything they did on the terminal was immediately relayed to the mainframe computer, they were afraid they would make fools of themselves in front of the technical people. Indeed, most people who first use a computer blame themselves for every problem – not the manuals, not the program, not the hardware. For example, once when I was using a terminal during my research study and made a careless mistake, the whole computer system crashed. I immediately ran to the computer room to ask what I had done wrong. Of course, I had not caused the crash – my error and the computer failure just happened to occur at the same time. With personal computers, the managers were able to make whatever mistakes they wanted – without anyone knowing.

Unmet needs

But, it is not just the fear of being made to look foolish or the belief that only typists (and other lower level workers) use keyboards that prevent large-scale adoption of information technology by executives. For most executives, the information technology just does not meet their needs. Executives can use information technology for three major purposes: as a wordprocessor, as a communication channel, and as information broker (all three of these uses are detailed in the following chapters). Many executives use the computer as a wordprocessor and communication vehicle; few use it to access information and support their decision making. Why? To answer this question, we first need to ask why the adoption of such technology is promoted. What are its perceived advantages by its creators and marketers? In general terms, a new technology is adopted if it improves technical efficiency and contributes to institutional stature. In other words, the company gains a competitive advantage.

Does information technology improve the *technical efficiency* of executives? Not very much. The most commonly proposed information technology for management is one that facilitates decision making. These decision-support systems assume that 'preferences are stable, problems and premises preceded solutions and conclusions, information is neutral and managers make decisions by considering alternatives in terms of their anticipated consequences for prior objectives' (March and Sproull 1990, p. 150). As we saw in Chapter 2, human information processing is far less structured. For example, imagine a decision-support system that controls managers' calendars. The manager provides the information for the programmer: times when she has regularly scheduled meetings or other engagements; a priority list of preferred times for meetings, for seeing individuals; a priority list of people; a priority list of projects/topics; the time length of different meeting types. An employee can log straight into the manager's calendar and attempt to set up a time to drop by. The program can even prompt the employee to name the topic to be discussed. The manager's secretary can do the same – but she has access to the calendars of other people and so can schedule a meeting without ever talking to any

of the principals. This sounds efficient, but what if the topic is delicate and can not be captured well in a few words in the topic
space? What about the employee who is ranked at the bottom of
the list? He will soon find out when he keeps trying to make an
appointment and finds there is never any time to see him. The
manager may never know he has been trying to see him until it is
too late. Certain conventions of face-to-face and telephone conversations are broken. Our cultural convention is to give an excuse
when refusing an offer or request. So, instead of the usual polite
excuse (even if untrue), the employee gets shut out of the calendar.
Another convention, that of serendipitous meetings, is flouted. As
mentioned earlier in the criticism of The Coordinator, many decisions are begun and made through happenstance, which is why
many good, experienced managers talk about 'walking the halls'
or 'the water cooler talk'. These are just a few of the problems in
what is really a very simple decision-support system. Imagine how
many more problems might arise when using a system to decide
whether to market a certain product or fire an employee. These
systems do not necessarily improve the technical efficiency of
the manager, largely because human decision making is not so
structured.

Decision-support systems have been fairly unsuccessful, largely
because of the changing information needs and decision criteria of
executives. Executives have a great need for information on which
to base their decisions. This information is gathered through their
staff and middle management, both through direct requests and
serendipitously. Why can a computer decision-support tool not
provide such information? First, the information the manager needs
changes daily and her preferences change with changing information and situations. To program a computer to support a calendar is
relatively trivial; to program one to constantly change the information base and the decision-making criteria is (certainly at present)
impossible. Even more fundamentally, decision-support programs
have been built on a biased set of information. Such a system (if
possible) would dramatically alter the balance of power in the executive suite. Staff (and especially bureaucrats) use their knowledge
to exert influence. Often the request for information that an executive makes is ill-formed, vague. The staff person is then able to
mould the reply such that it meets the request but also gives him
power in the decision-making process. In parliamentary countries,
such a system provides continuity, despite the change of elected

leaders. It is the public servant bureaucrat who guides decisions. Many, of course, would relish a system that took power away from such officials. But, they are unlikely to relinquish power easily. Further, it is the knowledge of the system that they control that may be invaluable to the decision-making process. Thus, if the programmer receives expert advice only from the executive, a large part of the necessary information base will be missing.

The other reason for adoption of a new technology is if it contributes to *institutional stature*. Does the calendar system enhance the manager's prestige and thus the image of his company? Not necessarily. While it may be viewed as efficient, it is probably also viewed as cold and inhuman. The executive has lost some of her 'charm' and 'people skills'. When other more complex decision-support systems are used, they are seen as removing the responsibility and control from the human being considered (by her very position) most capable of making the decisions. 'If managers believe that what makes them uniquely human (or managerial) is their role as decision makers, they will be slow to abdicate that uniqueness in favor of technology' (March and Sproull 1990, p. 156). Executives do not need help with decision making; they need help with gathering information. And, this could happen if executives used Computer-mediated Communication (CmC) to gather information from a broad base of employees (as Bill Gates of Microsoft does), and if they used appropriate information retrieval systems. But, as I showed above, these information systems may not provide the filtered and processed information the executive really needs.

So, it seems clear why executives have not rapidly adopted information technology for their own use, relying on their staff to access databases, to test ideas on computer simulations, or through decision-support systems. They keep for themselves the role of accessible leader and expert decision maker.

WHAT SKILLS FOR FUTURE WORKERS?

Many commentators on the information age and its effects on the workplace have focused on the need for workers who are more knowledgeable, have more skills and adaptability. They claim we will need a more educated workforce, not a less educated one. Raj Reddy, the head of the Robotics Institute at Carnegie-Mellon university, puts it this way:

> The old dogma of 'labor-value' theory is no longer relevant. It must be replaced by a 'knowledge-value' theory based on a symbiotic relationship between man [sic] and his personal computer providing access to the knowledge of the world. The value of a person or a society will be *directly proportional to their ability to master the information resource to achieve their goals.*
>
> (McCorduck 1985, p. 213, emphasis in original)

Fewer skills required

Interestingly, the example of the airline agents counters this trend to more knowledgeable workers who can access required information. Their entire job has been redefined by technology. They do need to be able to access the computer for information on schedules, fares, etc. But, they no longer need to have this information in their head as they did years ago. This is a perfect example of the computer performing a task that is highly complex. Computers can better store this information and change it when fares and schedules change. But no longer are the reservation agents communicators who hear what the customer wants and try to customize a flight schedule to fit that person's needs.

An even better example of workers needing less knowledge and skill can be seen when visiting a local McDonald's. The cash register, instead of having numbers on it, has symbols representing the various products. Thus, the server need only press the correct symbols and the price will appear. Similarly, even the chefs' duties are controlled by computers that assess the time to fry the french fries or the time to grill the meat patties. The chefs need make no judgements at all.

Greater skills required

At the other end of the scale are jobs that require literacy and understanding of the relationship between the computer and the product. We see the ever-increasing need for computer programmers, electronic engineers and systems analysts. The principles set out by Johnson and Rice show that more communication and skill at understanding one's job and articulating needs, problems and solutions are vital for successful information technologies. We can no longer afford to let systems be designed solely by systems analysts and implemented solely by management. We need to ensure that the technology fits well with the way people communicate and process information:

> Our need to make sense of an increasingly confusing world of men and machines often leads us to blur the distinction, first in the way we speak and then in the way we act. We anthropomorphize machines ('electronic brain') and we 'mechanomorphize' people ('What makes them tick?'), and we allow ergonomics, the philanthropic science of adapting machines to people, to merge into a darker science of adapting people to machines.
>
> (Simpson, 1984, p. 85).

Because of this frequent lack of fit of computer technology in the workplace, William W. Winspisinger, president of the International Association of Machinists and Aerospace Works, has suggested that there be a Technology Bill of Rights. It says:

1. New technology must be used in a way that creates and maintains jobs and promotes full employment.
2. New technology must be used to improve the conditions of work.
3. New technology must be used to develop the industrial base.
4. Workers and their trade unions must have a role in the decision-making processes with respect to the design, deployment, and use of new technology.

(McCorduck 1985, pp.. 211–212)

FOR DISCUSSION

1. If you had been trying to enquire about airline fares, like the grandmother in the scenario, how would you have responded? How would you have felt?
2. Technology is the combination of both the machine and the methods involved in its performance. Think of a technology that you have resisted using (e.g., computers, video-recording machines, a new software package, a different computer, a different function on a VCR). Why do you resist? What might be the advantages in using it? What might be the disadvantages?
3. If you were an employee whose manager used a calendar system such as that described earlier, how would you feel about that manager? What would you do to try to circumvent these controls and filters? How do you think she might improve the system to accommodate the criticisms I made against their use?

FOR ACTION

1. Observe a workplace (your own or a different one). What inter-actions/conversations are serendipitous and unplanned? What would be lost to people and the workplace if those conversations had not taken place?
2. Observe a workplace, different from the one you observed in point 1. Draw a network that shows the way information flows in this setting. What technologies are used in this information flow? Do they facilitate it or hinder it? How could they be improved?
3. Try to use a computer different from one you have ever used before. Take notes of what you do, what you think and what you feel. How did you work out the 'rules' for the computer – for its keyboard, its functions?

FURTHER READING

Garson (1988) gives detailed descriptions of the effect of computer-ization on different people and their jobs. Johnson and Rice (1987) examine the introduction of wordprocessing into the office, show-ing how to manage such organizational innovation. Goodman et al. (1990) provide a research agenda and theoretical framework for studying technology in organizations. Howard (1985) discusses the effects of information technologies on the workplace environment.

FOUR

The computer as phone message service

Most of us are now familiar with the telephone answering machine. Whether we have one ourselves or not, we call friends or businesses and are requested to 'leave a message after the beep' because they are not present or able or willing to answer the telephone. The use of such machines began over 20 years ago, with the one-way device. We called airlines, banks, public departments only to hear a message asking us to wait since all lines were busy; then, we heard music, almost always of a style or period we didn't like. After what seemed an interminable time, we were connected to a 'live' human being and were able to complete our interaction. Or, we called the local movie theatre and, instead of talking with the cashier, we heard a recorded message giving us the times of the movies. Such one-way communications still exist and have been expanded to provide multiple-choice menus for callers. In addition, we now have two-way systems in which the callee prepares a message telling the caller she is away from the telephone right now, but requesting the caller identify him or herself, the time and date of the message, leave a message and/or telephone number so the callee can call back later. This and subsequent messages from callers are stored on a tape recorder and played back at the convenience of the callee. A more recent development has been the use of a computer-based PBX (Private Branch Exchange) system by an entire organization, in which such 'voice mail' is stored centrally and is part of the telephone system; or we can buy such a service from our telephone company. In addition to storing messages, such systems allow us to forward calls (including appending our own message), broadcast the same message to more than one number, or conduct a conference call. Currently, voice mail is largely used in businesses; but a number of telephone companies began trials of a home voice mail service for the general public in 1988 and now this service is commonly available.

One-way voice mail is still used as in the following example:

Our university was given a large gift from Apple Computer, Inc. and, with several other faculty, I have written a number of grant proposals through which we have obtained equipment for three computer class-rooms for English Department instruction. There is one piece of software I have seen advertised in a professional journal, one that will help students respond to each other's drafts as they write their compositions. I call the Apple toll-free number in the advertisement. They know noth-ing about the availability of this software and suggest I call Customer Relations, a long distance call, A voice at the other end says: 'Thank you for calling Apple Customer Relations. If you're calling from a touch-tone telephone and your question is regarding applications software, please press 1 now. If your question is regarding an Apple promotional offer, please press 2 now. If you have a general question regarding Apple products, please press 3 now. I know not to talk to him since it's a recording. But, so much information is presented so quickly, I can not remember what the three options are. I choose the last in the hope that a real person will respond to general questions. After pressing 3, I get another recorded message, telling me I have reached Apple Customer Relations, that all the representatives are busy, but to please stay on the line as calls will be taken in order. The recorded message then says that if I am calling for technical support, I should call our nearest Apple Dealer. It then goes on to say in great detail how the dealer has access to Apple information and gives a toll-free number to call to find out the name and location of our nearest Apple Dealer. The message continues that if I want to speak with a customer relations representative (i.e. a real person) I should hold for the next available representative. Since I am not sure whether I made the first choice correctly, I hang up, redial and decide to press 1. I get another recorded message giving me a list of soft-ware products, none of which is the program I am interested in. I am also told that most of the software is now marketed by another company and am given their name, address, and telephone number. But, the advertisement I saw said it was an Apple product; so, I decide to hold and wait for a real person. After some time on hold, I speak with a rep-resentative who has also never heard of the program. After telling him where I read about it, he suggests I call the toll-free number. I quickly say that is how I got the number to call him! After much negotiation, he decides it must fall under the category of Higher Education Marketing and connects me to that department before I have time to ask for the actual number in case I get cut off. The telephone rings and I get a per-sonalized recorded message. He is out of his office. I leave a message asking him to call me back. He never calls. Every time I think of calling, I procrastinate because I know I will have to go through the sequence of recorded messages again since I do not have his number. A couple of

months later I decide to try again. This time, I look up the number for
Apple Computer, Inc. in the telephone directory and call their headquarters, get to talk with a real person, and she gives me the number of
the Higher Education Marketing person, who again is out of his office.
Fortunately for me, the calls to Customer Relations were in the next
telephone zone and so not too expensive. Also, I could use the telephone
directory since Apple is located close to our campus. I hate to think what
I would have done and what it would have cost if I had been calling
from the East Coast. Unfortunately this anecdote does not have a happy
ending. The program was developed with an Apple grant, but will not
be marketed by them. The writers, at the University of South Carolina,
are still looking for a software company to market their product.

While such a call may eventually get us the information we want,
it takes several minutes to get through the recorded messages
before we even have the opportunity to talk to a person. This
becomes especially frustrating if we are calling because we do not
know whom we should actually contact over a special problem.
The next example illustrates the time that can be wasted not only
through using such a system, but also as a result of the system.

Citizens chosen for possible jury service in our county suffer from such a
one-way message system. With the postal notification that I had been
called for possible jury service, I was given a time and telephone number
to call to get instructions about where to go. The number supplies a
recorded message that indicates the names (alphabetically) of those who
should go to the courthouse, and the time and date they should go. This
message does not allow the caller to connect with a real person at all. I
knew that I was exempt from jury duty (in fact was ineligible) since I
was not a citizen of the United States; however, I had to take time off
work, turn up at the courthouse, and wait through the usual lengthy
process of disqualification because the system did not allow for direct
human contact.

While this system is efficient from the point of view of a court with
limited resources, it breaks the usual conventions of conversations,
especially those of service encounters, where we expect the clerk to
listen to our request. The model of conversation that has been
employed here is one-way. The implementation of the system has
only viewed conversation from the point of view of the court –
what their telephonist wants to say to the customer. But, imagine
the following life-saving scenario:

It is 8am and in the small apartment in Osage, Iowa, the phone rings.
Clyde Ritter, a 73-year-old living alone does not answer. He has fallen

into a diabetic coma. Immediately, a dispatcher in the emergency police office gets a call alerting her to send help to Clyde Ritter. All through the use of a computerized voice mail system. Had Clyde been able to, he would have picked up the telephone and heard a computerized voice asking him 'Good Morning! Are you OK?' Had he replied 'yes' the computer would have hung up and dialled its next daily call. But, receiving no answer, it dials emergency and automatically alerts the police.

This innovative system makes use of a fairly non-interactive communication system, one that we might not like for other communications – how many of us like to respond to a computerized voice? But, in this case it is a vital and life-saving link for older folk living alone.

The telephone had already added the fact that participants do not need to be co-present in *space* to carry on a spoken conversation. The context of voice mail adds a new dimension to telephone communication – spoken conversations in which the participants are not co-present in *time*. What effect does this have on the way we communicate? This new dimension, while providing for some increased efficiency in communication, has affected the way conversations are organized and the way interpersonal relations (or tenor) are played out, and I shall deal with each of these issues below. However, both interact – the way conversations are organized affects interpersonal relations and the way people respond to a non-present audience affects the organization. Thus, I shall discuss both issues, but organize them around the two parties involved – the caller and the callee. I shall end the chapter by examining why voice mail, while popular, has limitations in acceptance and use.

THE CALLER'S PERSPECTIVE

The caller is faced with two different speech events in voice mail: recorded message and message left. The recorded message refers to both the individual greeting message left on the machine by the callee and the menu of options such as the example of Apple's system given at the beginning of the chapter. The message left refers to the message the caller leaves for the callee.

Recorded messages

Individual greeting

In regular telephone conversations, the ringing of the bell is the summons, the callee responds (but in the United States does not self-identify except in a business environment), the caller self-identifies, and the core of the conversation begins. With voice mail, the callee is expected to leave a recorded message that minimally identifies the telephone number called. Most people, however, leave additional information, which may include an excuse for not responding in person, instructions to the caller, and messages (e.g., 'think of peace'). To identify the number called, many people merely state the telephone number, others identify the name of the callee, others identify the name and place (e.g., 'You have reached the office of Denise Murray, Chair of Linguistics and Language Development'). Still others take this opportunity to create a different persona, such as in the elaborate dramatization in the following:

> Hi. This is Max Winter's office. Excuse me a moment. Yes, Mr. President, I'll do that right away. Well, as I was saying. Oh yes, Your Holiness, I'll be right there. As you can see, I'm busy right now, but if you'd like to leave your name and telephone number, I'll get right back to you.

The issue here is how much additional information is tolerated? My response to this recorded message was not to leave a message. Instead, I called the general office number and left a message with the secretary for Max to call me. No doubt I was not the only person who considered such a message as intrusive and a waste of time since after a few weeks Max changed his message to a more standard form. While it may be amusing to hear such a recorded message once, most people perceive that Max flouted Grice's maxims of both quantity and quality, and possibly even relevance. The caller then feels that the callee has the conversational floor for too long and, unlike in co-present conversations, usually can not interrupt. Some PBX systems allow the caller to override the recorded message, which is in effect, an interruption and taking of the floor by the caller. However, if the caller does not know the system, or the callee does not state the instructions on the recorded message, the caller has no option but to listen to the entire turn.

Of course, the callee is faced with a dilemma of exactly how to frame a message that has the potential of an infinite audience – some of whom are intimate friends and family, others of whom are acquaintances, yet others of whom are complete strangers. In more usual conversations, we tailor our language to suit the topic and the audience. But, with recorded messages, the identity of the incoming caller and his reason for calling are unknown.

Menu system

I mentioned above my frustrating experience with the menu-driven one-way voice mail system at Apple. The principle of menus and decision trees is an efficient (and cost-effective) way for the callee to handle incoming calls. For example, in Chapter 1, I related what happened when I called the Australian Consulate to request an application form to apply for a new passport. While it took some time to work through the menus, it was better than being 'on hold' while waiting for a person to answer my quick question. These systems can be effective for the callee, but less so for the caller, especially if they are not programmed well, as in my Apple example. Two aspects of the context affect the efficiency of the menu system: linearity and complexity. And, it is the interaction of these two forces that determines how effective such a system is.

Even the menu system of the Australian Consulate is not ideal. While it does allow the caller to opt out, press 0, and speak to a real human being at any point in the call, it does not have a similar capability of repeating any message. In other words, even though the menu system itself is branching, the caller's path through it is considered linear. Thus, if the caller does not hear all the menu options – because of static on the line or background noise at the caller's end or even human inability to process information quickly enough, the only way to play it again is to hang up, dial again (and this is a long distance call) and go through the menu system again.

If the program is very complex, offering elaborate choices (as in the Apple example), the caller is frustrated. Human beings in highly literate societies have limited memory for orally delivered information. These systems suffer the deficiencies of so many pre-programmed systems: the caller can not cancel, skip, or branch back; the keypad provides very limited ability to enter information and queries; and they are expensive if the call is long distance. Since one-way menu-driven voice mail is not an efficient information retrieval system, it is best used for simple choices, rather than elaborate ones and should always provide the caller with the ability to move in different directions – backwards to repeat or sideways to branch out of the entire system. To be really efficient, the menu should allow the caller to press a key (always the same key) at *any* point in the call and have the previous menu repeated and so on back as far as the caller needs.

Message left

Since the summons has been responded to, the turn is now the caller's, who can leave (or not) a message for the person called. It is precisely because of this ability that, for many types of communication, voice mail is more efficient than its real-time counterpart, telephone conversation or its written counterparts, a memo or note. If the calls are solely transactional, they can easily be done with voice mail. They do not get lost like memos; nor do they get distorted by a receptionist or secretary who does not fully understand the topic. So, in the workplace, voice mail is now often used in place of the inter-office memo. It also prevents the frustrations of telephone tag – when callers keep missing each other or one manager's secretary leaves a message with another manager's secretary and so on, with the two managers never actually getting to talk. With voice mail, we can dispense with that secretarial duty, leaving messages for each other through voice mail. Additionally, voice mail messages can be shorter than conversation since there is no need for phatic communication, the communication that maintains social cohesion but does not move the interaction along (e.g. 'How are things going?', 'What's the weather like out there?').

But it is exactly because of this lack of phatic communication that many people find such systems impersonal, and even frightening. To make our system at San José State more personal, the telephone company gave the disembodied female voice a name – Molly! It is interesting that most of the machine message servers are female. I wonder when we will progress beyond the stereotype of a female telephone operator. Even for those who find voice mail indispensable, there is the frustration of not being able to speak to a human being, especially if our call is special or urgent in some way. We can find ourselves bounced from one recorded message to another, finding ourselves in 'voice mail jail'.

Because some people find such systems impersonal, not all callers feel comfortable with leaving a disembodied message on an answering machine. For them, with the interpersonal cues missing, the interaction is at best a poor substitute for real conversation. So, we find the phenomenon of null calls (see Dubin 1987), those calls in which the caller does not leave a message, but hangs up. Dubin claims that in the early use of answering machines, people failed to leave a message because they were inhibited when they realized they were talking to a machine. Although the number of null calls has decreased over the years, she looked for an explanation of those that do occur by examining coping strategies used by successful callers. Successful callers overlook the machine and talk directly to the callee. These successful callers often use face-to-face strategies such as the identification expression 'I'm . . .', rather than 'This is . . .', the latter identifier being associated with telephone talk. With intimate personal callers, identifiers are often absent. Similarly, successful callers often address the person whose voice appears on the message. A caller who hears a message left by Simon on behalf of the entire household may say 'Hi Simon. Please tell Mary that . . . ,' acknowledging the speaker of the message, even though the caller knows any member of the household may actually listen to the stored calls.

CALLEE'S PERSPECTIVE

Voice mail systems give more control of communication to the callee, in fact in the workplace, replacing the secretary who screened unwanted calls. Before voice mail, while many people could and did ignore the call, most treated the summons as they would a 'Hey, Jim!' on the street or at the market. They would leave whatever they were doing and answer the summons. Indeed, the norm is to interrupt a face-to-face conversation to answer the telephone. With voice mail, the callee can have it both ways – ignore the summons, but still know who the call is from and what the message is. Many people use voice mail to filter calls, waiting until the person has identified themself before picking up the phone. This latter feature, however, only happens with the telephone answering machine, and is not currently possible with a PBX. In this way the callee can control whom she will speak to and when.

While voice mail does put more control in the hands of the callee than do regular telephone conversations, it also removes some of that control. I can no longer claim that 'I didn't get your message'. For, with voice mail, if someone leaves several messages and I do not respond, I give a clear message to the caller – I don't want to answer your call. Unlike e-mail (as we shall see in the next chapter), silence is negative. Many times, a caller who has left a message will call again within a couple of hours, and demand to know why their call was not answered! The responsibility to re-initiate the conversation falls to the callee.

In addition to losing some control over entering a conversation, callees also lose some control over the length of turns. Just as there are crashing bores in real-time conversations, there are voice mail users who, uninterrupted by impatient noises or closing attempts by the other person, talk on and on seemingly endlessly, when the meat of the matter could have been given in a few sentences. In other words, these callers flout Grice's maxim of quantity by giving more information than is necessary. Of course, it is more difficult for us to gauge the background knowledge of the callee if we do not hear back channel responses such as 'Yes, I know'. 'Oh, fine.'

In good voice mail systems, we can jump forward and get through such calls fairly quickly; however, it is still inconvenient since we are never quite sure when the crux of the message will come. The first thing I do when I get to my office each day is to listen to the calls in my mailbox. When I hear certain voices, I inwardly cringe, knowing that I am in for a long message. Other people, without the usual non-linguistic cues, rush on at a speed that makes their message (and especially their telephone number) impossible to understand on one hearing only. Then, the callee is forced to repeat the message (sometimes several times) before getting the number down. Another major disadvantage (not shared by electronic mail, as we shall see in the next chapter) is that we have to take notes while listening to the message and then refer to the notes when replying, unless the message is extremely short or we have especially good memories. If the person is on the same voice mail system, I can, however, reply to each message immediately by pressing one key on the keypad. Also, people often forget to leave a telephone number or name, making replying difficult or impossible. And then they get angry because we have not responded with the second part of the adjacency pair (answering their question, for example). Thus, along with the increased control of some aspects of conversation, comes increased responsibility to identify the caller and message and reply.

WHY LIMITATIONS?

While voice mail has become extremely popular in countries with reliable and relatively inexpensive telephone services, it has not become as popular as one might expect. One major reason is that it changes the way we communicate and many people are still acquiring these new conventions. Another reason is that the technology is based on the metaphor of 'mail', which so far has prevented the technology from truly innovative applications.

Acquiring voice mail conversational conventions

Many of the problems associated with voice mail (or answering machines) are the result of lack of familiarity with the medium. Lack of familiarity results primarily from people making calls *to* voice mailboxes, but never *receiving* voice mail messages. This is rather like a child acquiring the first language and only ever speaking to people, never listening. Since interactional rules are acquired through two-way interaction these one-way callers do not acquire voice mail skills. People who do not leave telephone numbers soon learn to do so once they have voice mail themselves. As voice mail becomes more popular for home use, we will find people adapting their language use to the medium, just as proficient writers adapt their oral language to the written medium. After using the system for only a year, I found I was far more conscious of speaking clearly, concisely, and giving my name and telephone number slowly.

The mail metaphor

Because of the metaphors voice mail and voice mail box, users and technologists alike have a restricted vision of the potential of voice mail. Regular mail is delivered to an address rather than to a person. This is, of course, a physical constraint of hand-carried paper. So, too, my voice mail is delivered to a specific address (telephone number). Of course, using various access codes, I can call into my mail box and retrieve my messages from any other telephone. But, I have to call the main number at the office, listen to a greeting, enter my extension, and then enter my passcode before I can hear my stored messages. Since telephones are computerized, there is no technical reason why people can not have an individual code, one they take with them everywhere they go. This could be in the form of a computer card, which could then be plugged into any telephone anywhere. Thus, all my calls could be routed to me on that telephone. This feature is available on a single PBX, but, so far, telephone companies have not cooperated to develop a portable system whereby identification is by person, not by location. Or, it could be that I carry my telephone everywhere I go and, on reaching a new location, dial in to identify the region. Then I could receive calls directly. Motorola is working on a cellular phone system that might do this, a technically more difficult solution than the former.

The analogy to postal mail may also help explain why some implementations have such complex menu systems – they are based on a written culture, where people can scan back and forth until they have the information they need.

While people are adapting to this medium of communication, from the variety of message types it is clear that no norm or genre has yet emerged. For some (and I count myself among these), voice mail and answering machines are an efficient method for doing business and therefore the language style is professional, informative, but friendly. For others, talking to a machine is, at best, a poor substitute for person-to-person talk and therefore they excessively humanize their language style. And then there remain those who continue to feel discomforted and intimidated by a machine recorder. Many of the problems can also be overcome with more action research that identifies people's attitudes to different voice mail systems. Unfortunately, so much of the research conducted in the name of human factors is experimental and looks only at time and cost efficiency, not at people's responses as human beings or at the way we conduct conversations or service encounters with other people.

FOR DISCUSSION

1. How do recorded messages reflect the persona of the person who makes them?
2. How much time should a caller leave before making a second call? Why?

FOR ACTION

1. Call a company that has a voice mail menu system. Transcribe the messages. Draw a diagram to represent the branching of the

menu. Is this the most efficient system for these choices? What other menu could be used?

2. If you have voice mail, transcribe several messages left on your machine. What are the similarities and differences among them? How do they reflect the caller?

3. Develop a brief survey on voice mail (ask about 5–8 questions). You may want to ask questions about attitudes to and uses of voice mail. Survey five people. Compare the results. What advice would you give a voice mail company based on your small sample?

(Note: There is no further reading for this chapter since very little has been published.)

FIVE

The computer as communication site

Communication through language takes place in a variety of communication sites with which we are all familiar – face-to-face, the telephone, letters, books, etc. The computer adds another site to our repertoire, one that has a profound effect on the way we use language. This chapter focuses on the most interactive and immediate of computer communications, while Chapter 6 will deal with its wordprocessing function. The scenarios that follow illustrate the range of human-human interaction using the computer.

Imagine sitting down at your computer at noon Christmas Eve in San José, typing in your Christmas letter, pressing a key and sending it to your mother in Australia, friends in London, godchild in New Zealand, friends in a caravan park in a small Welsh village, a friend in Tokyo, and another in Athens, Greece. All with a few keystrokes. No worrying about the timing of a telephone call because of different time zones. No last minute visit to the Post Office and standing in line to buy more stamps or to mail letters you know will not arrive until after Christmas. Your letter to your mother arrives on her computer at 6am Christmas day, Australian time. When she gets up Christmas morning, she goes to her computer and reads your letter. Some time later the friend in Tokyo and the godchild in New Zealand read their e-mail, then the friends in England and Wales, followed by the friend in Greece. Meanwhile, you have read all their Christmas greetings on Christmas morning in California.

While some people will consider that sending the same electronic letter to all and sundry is a depersonalized Christmas greeting, this clearly demonstrates the potential of electronic mail, a potential that is still unrealized, as we shall see later in this chapter, because there are no international standards for such electronic communication, unlike the standards for postal mail, telegraph, telephone, telex and, more recently, fax (electronically transmitted facsimile). Or, imagine the following:

Arthur Pool, an Australian working for IBM wanted to bid for the computer installation at the University of Queensland in Brisbane. With 18,000 students, it is one of the largest in the country – a great market opportunity. But, to make the bid (and the final product) successful, the IBM mainframe computer would have to work in conjunction with several smaller systems and work stations manufactured by Digital Equipment Corporation, a competitor. Pool sent out a plea over IBM's internal CmC network (called VNET). Responses came back, scrolling in at the rate of dozens a day for several months, resulting in 500 pages of e-mail. Pool (and IBM) won the business.

Republican field organizers in the 1984 Reagan campaign used microcomputers to speed up campaign decision making. As one Republican official described it: 'When the [campaign] plane landed at one stop, you would get to a telephone and download your messages [from the headquarters computer to your microcomputer]. In the plane en route to the next city you could read and analyse the electronic mail. At the next stop, you were prepared to upload the answer, instructions, or strategy to another location.'

(Abramson et al. 1988, pp. 95–6)

During the 1992 Los Angeles riots, what started as an all-white electronic exchange on a bulletin board, venting anger against blacks and Latinos, turned into a fund-raising drive and consciousness raising for many contributors to the bulletin board. The change was sparked by a young black woman from South Central Los Angeles, who, protected by the anonymity of the bulletin board (where pseudonyms are widely used) engaged in critical discussions about race relations and joblessness with whites she would never had had the courage or opportunity to talk with and work with.

(Wallace 1992, pp. 8E and 15E)

A 27-year-old Chinese graduate student at Stanford University sits at a computer terminal, sending messages of support to the students protesting 6,000 miles away in Tiananmen Square in Beijing. He gathers information from the US news media and from friends and colleagues in China and relays informational bulletins to about 15 other cities throughout China, cities that cannot themselves find out directly what is happening in Beijing. Fax provides the information link, taking news from Beijing to other Chinese cities via US universities. It is now the 5th of June and this same student receives a BITNET message from a fellow Chinese student in San Diego, which reads

We just received a phone call from Beijing.
The caller is living near Mou-Xue-De where most killing happened.
1) The killing is MUCH MUCH worse than you can think of. The bullet is explosive kind (Zha4 Zi3). Five of his neighbours were killed

while sleeping at home. . . . (Taken from actual e-mail.)
The eyewitness report goes on to describe the massacre at Tiananmen Square.

These five scenarios demonstrate the increasing move away from stand-alone machines to computers that are networked together so that workers, colleagues and friends can talk to each other and send information to each other electronically. The networks connecting computers act as modern-day mail workers, collecting, carrying and distributing mail and other information across towns, states, countries, and the world. And, they act as a meeting or conference room, where people can share information and respond to each other in real-time and also asynchronously.

Since many futurists are envisaging the office becoming a community of telecommuters, we have to ask the question of whether remote communication among people will have disadvantages. While computer-mediated communication (CmC) can clearly perform a number of important functions in the workplace and even socially, can it substitute for daily face-to-face interaction with co-workers and friends, in terms of satisfying the social and emotional needs of participants, as well as their task-completion needs? Can it provide the cohesion and motivation necessary to coordinate work efforts? What effect does such a medium of communication have on language and social life? How are we adapting a written medium to an essentially oral communication style? How are traditional face-to-face behaviours altered? And, then, how can we utilize such communication systems to facilitate rather than impede human communication? Intimately bound up in all these questions are the very metaphors used to describe the various functions of the computer as communication vehicle, metaphors that make inaccurate comparisons among what are really quite different technologies and thereby limit the potential of the new technologies.

THE PROLIFERATION OF COMPUTER-MEDIATED COMMUNICATION (CmC)

Before discussing the effects and potentials of CmC, I want to demonstrate its increasing importance in certain communities.

Computer-mediated communication grew out of brief online messages sent from programmers at terminals to operators at terminals simultaneously logged onto the same mainframe computer.

These messages might be to request the operator to mount a tape or for the operator to inform people he was closing the computer down. This simple messaging facility allowed, or was soon extended to allow, all logged on users to send messages to each other. Next, the ability to transmit files of data was added. If the user was not logged on, the system held the file and presented it to the receiver when he next logged on. Originally, this feature was intended to facilitate the exchange of computer programs and data, but, since a file can contain text, electronic mail (e-mail) was born. The final step occurred when two computers (or more) were connected together in a network, allowing messages and files to be exchanged between users on different machines.

In many non-instructional settings, electronic mail (e-mail) is a major use of the computer – as of May 1989, North America had approximately six million mailboxes; in 1993 there were 42.3 million e-mail users worldwide (*San José Mercury News*, 24 June 1993, p. 21A). In my 1986 study of the use of computer-mediated communication within IBM, for example, I found that 86 per cent of the 150 users surveyed spend more than 10 per cent of their working week using the computer as a tool for communication while 28 per cent spend more than 30 per cent of their time on CmC. This is supported by Halpern's study (Halpern and Liggett 1985, p. 163) that found her 27 interviewees 'spend nearly twice as much of their time using electronic media as using conventional, such as pencil, pen, or typewriter'. When John Scully, then CEO of Apple Computers was on sabbatical, a mandatory requirement within the corporation, he checked his e-mail from home each day. IBM's new CEO, Louis V. Gerstner, has a published ID (see Glossary) on e-mail and daily receives hundreds of messages, replying to general themes by sending e-mail to all 250,000 workers. Both the President and Vice President of the United States have e-mail addresses and aides respond, just as they have traditionally responded to traditional mail. Within companies that have used e-mail for some time, workers talk of e-mail 'withdrawal', the feelings they have when on a business trip and not able to log onto a terminal to get their e-mail. Those on business trips to other centres often head straight to the nearest computer terminal, log on, and check their mail, whereas in previous times they headed for the telephone. As e-mail is becoming more popular with the general public, some people become constant 'chatterers', typing in to different e-mail and bulletin board services.

At home, we can now have access to public subscription electronic mail services such as MCI mail and America Online if we have a computer and a modem. In countries such as France, the Mini-Tel system is fast taking the place of an inefficient postal service. One such French user living in New York chats with other French people in France – a professional gambler, a film maker, a doctor, a marketing executive, and others. 'All of the sudden, here were all these people I could talk to at home, in my pajamas. I was hooked. But I couldn't really describe it to people. I mean, it's like, how do you describe chocolate?' (Sachs 1987, pp. 1A and 6A.) And, people are beginning to use portable computers with modems and cellular phones to access e-mail and transmit data anywhere at any time, even when travelling.

E-mail is also being used in instruction, as in the following scenario:

> Each school morning, two students in Betty Aten's fifth/sixth grade class at Taft School in Redwood City turn on the Apple IIe in their classroom and check the mail. Their 'mailbox' is part of a Bulletin Board System (BBS) located miles away at the San Mateo County Office of Education in Redwood City [California]. The girls use a special name and password to access the system and read the mail addressed to them and other students in their class from students in other schools. . . Later that same day, or maybe the next, their class will answer the letters they receive and thus 'telecommunicate' with their friends.
>
> (Scarola, 1986, pp. 1F and 6F)

This scene is replicated in cities across the United States and countries around the world, with students accessing computer networks to 'talk' with their electronic penpals.

Almost all computer services supplying information (such as CompuServe) or services and merchandise (such as Prodigy) also provide e-mail, often free. Networks interconnect the mainframe computers and campus networks of hundreds of colleges and universities in the United States and abroad. The networks and their acronyms multiply from ARPANET, the earliest academic and research network, established in 1969, to Internet, of recent (1988) fame when a Cornell computer hacker student planted a computer virus that multiplied and closed down hundreds of computers and networks within the Internet. Through these networks, in addition to e-mail and bulletin boards, users in one institution can log-in to another institution's computer to access specialized databases, statistical analysis packages, and online library catalogues. As I write in early 1994, the Vice President of the United States, Al Gore, is promoting the concept of the information superhighway, a network of computer services that would include multiple television channels (predictions are around 500), shopping, music that could be transmitted directly into the home, bulletin boards, and e-mail. However, what many of the supporters of the information highway overlook is what function will people most want to use the superhighway for? As mentioned above and in the introduction, the advent of computers in homes and businesses has shown that people mostly want to communicate—not shop or even watch TV. All the commercial uses in the United States have been little used. Online services such as Prodigy have not made great profits; nor has home purchasing via TV. Computer technology in fact mirrors print technology:

> We do not write and read [or use computers] primarily in order to ensure this nation's employers can count on a competent, competitive work force. We write and read in order to know each other's responses, to connect ourselves more fully with the human world, and to strengthen the habit of truth-telling in our midst.
>
> (DeMott 1990, p. 6)

So, too, with computers. We need to see them as a means for humans to connect with each other and each other's ideas, not just a tool for commercialism. And networks and e-mail provide us with that opportunity.

Many futurists are predicting the office of the future will be the home or just where the person happens to be at the moment, since many people will telecommute, made possible through networks such as those I have just mentioned. In their 1978 book, *The Network Nation*, Hiltz and Turoff predicted that computerized conferencing would be a prominent form of communication in most organizations by the mid-1980s and that by the mid-1990s, it would be as widely used in society as the telephone was in 1978. While their dramatic forecasts have not come to pass (see my discussion later in this chapter), CmC has proliferated and is continuing to do so.

VARIETIES OF CmC

Let me first describe the various ways in which people can communicate with each other via the computer, that is, through CmC. CmC refers here to any human–human communication mediated directly via a computer, including the following modes, listed in order from the mode with the most potential for immediate interaction to the mode with the least.

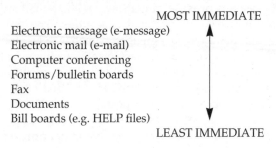

MOST IMMEDIATE

Electronic message (e-message)
Electronic mail (e-mail)
Computer conferencing
Forums/bulletin boards
Fax
Documents
Bill boards (e.g. HELP files)

LEAST IMMEDIATE

Electronic messages (e-message)

E-message refers to the interchange of messages between two or more participants simultaneously logged onto computer terminals. The actual structure of these messages varies among different computer systems – some are like CB and allow only one person to 'talk' at a time; others restrict the length of the message; most do not store the messages. The example below is from IBM's VM system, which restricts the length of messages.

MSG FROM PARK(BRIAN): any particular reason you sent me XEDITG?
VMSG PARK(BRIAN): so latest version can be placed on public park disk
MSG FROM PARK(BRIAN): ok will do it now

Not all commercial services have this feature. In those that do, people can form chat rooms, talking about subjects of interest such as parenting or politics.

E-mail

E-mail allows people to type extended messages at computer terminals and have those messages electronically transmitted to recipients who can read, reply, delete, print, forward, or file them. The sender can keep a copy in a computer file. Like e-messages, the form e-mail takes varies with the computer system. The most primitive requires both sender and receiver to have their modems and computers turned on simultaneously and both need a communications package to transmit and receive the data. The second approach is the most common, where people use an intermediary as electronic mailbox. Services such as CompuServ, MCI Mail, AT&T Mail, America Online and BITNET provide such electronic mailboxes, which act as storage bins for mail. Most popular local area network (LAN) systems provide similar messaging, e-mail and mailbox facilities for networks of personal computers. The third approach allows the sender to send e-mail to someone who does not have a computer. In this case, the service prints out the e-mail on a printer at a location that is close to the e-mail's destination, rather than storing it in the electronic mailbox. The printed version of the e-mail is then delivered by courier or postal service. Since the first and third approaches do not involve interactive communication, I will focus on the second and most popular e-mail approach, that of electronic mailboxes.

The e-mail example below is from a systems support person from my university, replying to a question I had sent him through e-mail. As you can see, our userids (electronic addresses) are a somewhat random collection of numbers and letters. Mine is TFCAAK9. I have inserted my name, which appears on all e-mail sent to or from me using my userid. My question was how to access a file that came via BITNET but was too long to be called up through MAIL.

Message 4, Page 1 of 2

- -

```
Date:     Thu, 30 Apr 1987 09:04 PDT
From:     <TGCONSL> (cc sjsu)
Subject:  file in wt queue
To:       <TFCAAK9> (Denise Murray)
```

this is regarding the file in your wait queue. try the following:

    1. enquire,jsn

this should tell you the jsn of the file that is in your wait queue.

    2. qget,jsn,fn=fname

this gets the file from your wait queue and makes it local under the supplied filename

    3. replace,fname

this saves your local copy

to read the file you may have to specify "ascii" and then list it.

nb:

  in #2 you substitute the jsn you got from the list in #1.

  good luck and you can reach me here at tgconsl on ccs.

In many systems, the subject line is automatically provided and the sender may or may not choose to fill in the subject. In some systems that use line editors rather than full-screen editors, the system prompts the sender with 'subject?' People new to such systems often do not see this prompt and begin typing their letter at the subject prompt. Consequently, part of their message appears in the subject line, part is missing (since the subject line has a restricted length), and the rest is in the usual letter section. The following is an example of e-mail (with details changed for anonymity) I received from a colleague who sent her e-mail via America Online. The sytem provided her userid, the America Online identification, the identification of the actual e-mail. Sharon provided the subject when prompted by the computer, which also inserted the subject at the end of the message.

From: sharon@aol.com
X-Mailer: American Online Mailer
Sender "sharon" <sharon@aol.com>
Message-Id <9402152308.tn232275@aol.com>
To: murray%sjsuvm1.bitnet@cmsa.Berkeley.EDU
Date: Tue, 15 Feb 94 23:08:18 EST
Subject Affiliate Workshop

I've finally heard from Tom – I thought he had gotten in touch with you
before now. We are able to switch you to 3:20–3:50. It will be in Stouffers
Maryland Ballroom B. (Actually, the small groups will be meeting in different
rooms possibly, which I don't know yet – I'll let you know). I guess this
is your formal notice on this – do you mind not getting a letter? I will
attend your session and help if you need it. I know you will be very aware
of how to address an audience of affiliate leaders!

Affiliate Workshop

The following e-mail (using pseudonyms), shows how users can have personalized userids and customize the header to include the phone number, and even the postal address. MARY is Mary

Wallace's userid and PARK indicates the address of the actual computer.

Date: 7 March 1992, 15:38:54 PST
From: MARY WALLACE   MARY at PARK 777–7777
       Systems Information
       Computer Company
       1200 Disk Drive
       Silicon Valley, CA 0000
To: PHILK at ELCAMINO
Subject: questionnaire

Phil:
I cannot locate some of the folk you mentioned who might
make useful comments on my questionnaire as follows:

Ben Schmidt – can't locate at all (CJNTEL)
David Goldberg – dept & bldg in EC directory but no USERID
Trent Gorden – can't locate at all (CJNTEL or research directories)

Do you know their locations (and preferably USERIDs)?

Thanks,
Mary.

Computer conferencing/fora/bulletin boards/newsgroups

Because CmC is a new and evolving form of communication, different systems offer different permutations and combinations of the types of communication. Moreover, the exact same type can have a different name in a different system. Bulletin boards, newsgroups, or fora are usually services where people can add messages and respond to other people's message. They are rather like an extended set of e-mail messages, except that they are often anonymous. They are a constantly updated collection of hundreds (and thousands) of postings, usually on a given subject. Some systems call this form of communication a computer conference.

Computer conferencing in most systems refers to a facility in which more than two people can communicate with e-messages, e-mail, bulletin boards and documents, usually for a specific purpose. EIES (Electronic Information Exchange System), for example, includes e-mail, asynchronous and synchronous conferencing, notebooks and bulletin boards. Most computer conferencing facilities require participants to be members of the conference, which can usually be done simply by requesting addition to the conference (and paying the service and use fee if it is a commercial computer conference). The conference stores all the e-messages, e-mail and documents for access by conference participants. In most systems, e-messages, e-mail and documents are stored separately and in temporal order. The major difference between a computer conference and e-mail is that in e-mail, the sender specifies who will receive the correspondence; in a conference, everyone with access to the conference can read all contributions to the conference. Most conference systems, however, provide e-mail as well, to allow for what is called 'whispering', that is, sending private messages to some conferees without the others knowing a side conversation is going on.

The university system of which San José State is a part, has a conferencing system and a bulletin board system. The latter is actually a bill board since it is used solely for announcements. People wanting to make comments on the notices have to do so using the appropriate conference or by sending e-mail directly to the person responsible. When I log on to this system, I get the following message:

ATL BULLETIN BOARD MAIN MENU

(a) ATL News and Information
(b) Requesting an Account
(c) Computer Conferencing
(d) UNIX system including (Writer's Workbench)
(e) Look at ATL Bulletin Boards
(f) ATL Help and System Information
(g) ATL Mail
(q) Quit the menu system

Please enter your choice:

If I want to check one of the conferences on which I am a member, I choose (c) and receive the following message:

```
You have 2 mail message(s) in your in-basket,
You are a member of 4 conference(s)
From      Memo  *  Date
hbrown    1348R      Mon Jan 30 15:09 1989. 2nd yr funding
hbrown    1461R      Tue Mar 7  15:25 1989. travel money
To        Memo  *  Date
You have no conv. msgs.
Conf/Topic          New Messages
Learn/general          22
api/general             1
```

This tells me I have two e-mail messages waiting for me. One is old (about second year grant funding), but is still in my basket since I specified that it not be deleted. The learn/general conference is one for learning how to use the system and so always has many new postings. The conference 'api/general' has only one new posting, so I decide I want to read it. I type the command to access that conference and am automatically taken to the first entry I have not already read. Or, I could ask to read the first (or any other) item in the conference. When I choose 'first', the following appears on my screen:

```
........................................................................
api/general #1, from ttang , 445 chars Mon Oct 3 21:27:54 1988
........................................................................


  TITLE: greeting
    Hello, everyone! This is your friendly Conference Moderator. I have
  just finished entering your names as participants in our api conference.
  I did not receive your userid's and password until late this afternoon,
  Monday, October 3. This does not give me much time to get ready for
  our workshop at Cal Poly on Thursday, October 6. See you at their
  spanking new training laboratory, and please bear with me.

  Thanks.



    No more unread messages on this topic
    Hit <RETURN> for next active conf/topic


  [_____]                              O O O  [][]
```

As we can see in Tom's append to the api conference, he is the
conference moderator. Most conferences have a moderator who
answers questions about computer use, arranges for people to
become members of the conference and assigns them passwords
and userids if required.

Documents

Documents include memos, the minutes of meetings, reports and
technical papers, that have formatting controls designed for printing. They may be sent to recipients in hard copy (printout), the
recipient may be sent a formatted copy for reading online, or the
recipient may be sent an unformatted copy that may be read online
or formatted and printed locally. This is the wordprocessing function of the computer and will be discussed in detail in the next
chapter. The potential for immediate participation is restricted
unless the sender is asking for feedback, in which case the recipient
may append, annotate or otherwise comment on the document.

Fax

Fax gained international reputation during the 1989 Tiananmen Square massacre in The People's Republic of China. Fax (short for electronically transmitted facsimile) translates the image on a piece of paper into a code, which is sent electronically over telephone lines to the receiving fax machine, which in turn converts the code into an image of the original piece of paper, and prints the copy. The typical fax machine is a dedicated device containing a scanner for converting printed images into digital form, a modem for sending and receiving the data, and a printer.

Bill boards

Bill board refers to the online distribution of information. This can include schedules, cafeteria menus, consumer services such as Prodigy (see Glossary), and news. In general, most users can access bill boards to retrieve information, but not to insert information. Since this form of CmC is not truly interactive and relies on the user being able to interface with predetermined messages on the computer screen, it will be discussed in Chapter 7.

This chapter will focus on the conversations produced through e-messages, e-mail, bulletin boards and computer conferences. These conversations are only just beginning to have the impact that futurists such as Hiltz and Turoff predicted. Rather, the less interactive fax has caught the public's attention. So, I will also discuss the interactive uses of CmC in the light of fax.

THE EFFECTS OF CmC ON COMMUNICATION

This new communication site, because of its technical characteristics, has resulted in new ways of using language, in new ways of organizing communication, and new ways of interacting. CmC is being used increasingly in education; however, I will confine the discussion here primarily to non-educational settings. The discussion is organized around the major issues concerning interactive communication via computer:

- What does the language of CmC look like?
- How does CmC change the way people interact?
- How do people fit this new medium into their repertoire of means of interaction?

The changes to language and interaction simplify communication, but at the same time cause ambiguities. They free participants from the constraints of 'normal' conversational rules, removing some of the barriers to open communication (such as power), but at the same time removing some of the constraints that make for 'polite' conversations. In the business environment, the focus of communication is on transactions (as described by the conversation for action theory discussed in Chapter 2). The simplification and freedom of CmC facilitate this focus. But, another aspect of CmC hinders efficient transactions – how to file and store it – do you file under topic, under date, under name of sender? In other settings, such as education and public bulletin boards, we find that the same ambiguities and freedoms inhibit communication. Even in the business world, we find that some people want to exercise more control, leading to the development of programs such as The Coordinator described in Chapter 3.

How does the computer affect the language of CmC?

One of the first characteristics that strikes new users of CmC is the blurring of the distinction between talk and text. In CmC, talk is electronic text and text is interactive, resulting in different clusters of surface linguistic features.

The language of CmC is a simplified register, a hybrid of oral and written language. Users simplify their language in order to meet their primary goal of interactive communication within a context that has a different grouping of constraints from those of oral or written language. Typing at a terminal is slower than speaking; time delays occur also because of technical failures; the recipient is not physically present and so CmC has no visual paralinguistic or non-linguistic cues. The grouping of contextual features of CmC is also different from that of casual conversation or of any of the well-studied simplified registers described in Chapter 2. Unlike caretaker talk and foreigner talk, but like notetaking, the audience has full language competence while constrained by time and space. Thus, the simplification strategies that CmC communicators use all serve to reduce the time taken to write the message or to substitute for paralinguistic and non-linguistic cues.

Reducing time

To reduce the time, computer communicators abbreviate, simplify lexis and syntax, and disregard surface errors. But, at the same time, they maintain Grice's maxim of quantity, that is, to say as much as is needed to be understood, but no more.

ABBREVIATIONS

Abbreviations include those commonly used in everyday life (e.g., 'tonite'); phonetic spelling (e.g., 'u r' for 'you are' and 'ur' for 'your'); extension of the meaning of computer commands (e.g., 'c/weds./tues/' meaning to change wed to tues in a previous message); and acronyms (e.g., 'F2F' for 'face-to-face'; 'BRB' for 'be right back'; 'BTW' for 'by the way' and 'YW' for 'you're welcome').

CmC, note-taking and caretaker talk all use abbreviation as a simplification strategy. However, the use of phonetic spelling, lexical extension, or phrasal acronyms used in CmC are not used in any other studied simplified register. CmC, then, employs the same strategy but extends and expands its use.

LEXICAL SIMPLIFICATION

Other simplified registers (foreigner talk and caretaker talk) employ lexical modification. Foreigner talk upgrades language by replacing slang with standard lexical items; caretaker talk separates reduced casual forms. CmC, on the other hand, uses casual style to discuss highly technical topics.

SYNTACTIC SIMPLIFICATION

Syntactic simplification involves many of the features of other simplified registers. Like note-taking talk, the writers preserve inflections for tense and number. Caretaker talk and foreigner talk, on the other hand, simplify by dropping inflections. These strategies differ because the audience is different. Both note-takers and CmC readers have full language competence; simplification is due to time and space constraints, not language competence. Syntactic simplification includes deletion of subject, auxiliary, copula, subject and verb, and sometimes of determiner.

Other simplified registers also use deletion. For example, note-taking talk and foreigner talk delete the subject, whereas caretaker talk uses pronoun shift (e.g., the use of 'we' or the child's name instead of 'you') as a clarifying device. However, CmC register uses a greater variety of deletion; but, like caretaker and foreigner talk, often retains articles, even when they are not vital to understanding. In CmC, deletion also occurs in question formation, where its use is extensive. Questions are very common in CmC and mostly rely on the use of the question mark to indicate interrogative. This is similar to the use of rising intonation on a statement in caretaker talk and foreigner talk. Deletion can include all parts of the verb, modals, or 'do' plus subject, resulting in language such as:

> (do you) have a minute for a question?
> (have you had) ANY FURTHER WORD FROM STEVENS?
> (shall) I CALL?

DISREGARD FOR SURFACE ERRORS

Since CmC (and e-messages especially) is composed on the fly, the goal is communication rather than formal accuracy. Thus, typos and infelicities of syntax are ignored unless ambiguous. The following example clearly demonstrates how CmC users, like speakers in oral conversation, do not self-correct unless miscommunication is likely. This example also illustrates subject/verb deletion, acronym use and abbreviations.

> P1: I can;t find Don, Simon or Les logged on.
>   Where are people going for coffee?
> M1: no idea. i haven't seen a sole all day. btw can i do
>   foils on yourprofs sys on sun?

This disregard for surface errors can perhaps be seen as similar to the almost ungrammatical language used in foreigner talk (e.g., 'not happen' for 'doesn't happen'). Since communication is the goal in each case, the standard conventions of spoken and written language are not necessarily maintained.

Substituting for paralinguistic and non-linguistic cues

SYMBOLIZATION

Symbolization is used primarily to represent paralinguistic and non-linguistics cues since these forms of communication are not available in CmC. Symbolization includes markers such as the following:

> – expressives e.g., 'humpf' and 'pshaw'
> – '"*text*"': asterisks to indicate emphasis as in
>   "i *did* say users(still and i got back no!"

- Multiple vowels for rising intonation e.g., "sooooo"
- Multiple "?" or "!" to indicate affect e.g., "well how did things go
      yesterday????"
- icons/smileys/emoticons such as ":<(" for a sad face.

Asterisks were originally used for stress because the more traditional upper case could not be used since e-messages were
converted to upper case by the computer system. With the introduction of mixed case e-messages, upper case is often used for
emphasis; however, many users continue to use the asterisks that
have become so conventionalized.

The use of symbolization is also shared with note-taking talk
(e.g., '+' for 'and'). The use of orthographic paralinguistic cues to
represent expression is paralleled by the expressive processes of
both caretaker talk and foreigner talk, which use diminutive, exaggerated stress and intonation to convey such effect.

For most people, this simplified register makes CmC both interactive and time effective – it has the immediacy and casualness of
face-to-face and telephone conversations, without their need for
phatic communication and other characteristics of conversations
that focus on interaction. For others, its very brevity appears impersonal.

How does CmC affect the way people interact?

As we saw in Chapter 2, conversation is regulated by sociocultural conventions such as turn-taking and appropriacy of style,
conventions resulting from the context. Since the context of CmC
is different from that of other contexts, we find different conventions for conducting CmC conversations. These differences are
found in the organization of conversation and in interpersonal
relations.

Organization of conversation

Just as users simplify their language to accommodate the constraints of the medium, so too they have developed different norms
for the organization of conversations – the turn-taking is complex,
adjacency pairs are often absent, as are opening and closing moves,
and conversations contain a number of content threads.

TURN-TAKING

Because of the time delay in CmC, e-messages, e-mail, or bulletin board contributions cross each other and overlap. In face-to-face and telephone conversations one party usually speaks at a time (although this does differ across cultures). But, in CmC the sender may send a second e-message, e-mail, or bulletin board contribution before receiving a response to the first. This difference is most dramatic in the interactive e-message or chat, where an e-message may even interrupt a turn, as the following example tellingly illustrates:

> T1: THEY HAVE IT RUNNING DOWN AT THE LAB (ON SYS21)
> P1: yeah – using lab 'f' for home terminal support i bet!
> T1: ALSO ON SYS24. ISN'T IT SOMETHING?
> P2: what would be the effect of having the home term
>   with ymon using a high speed modem?
> T2: ALEX WAS INTERESTED IN PUTTING IT UP ON SYS54
> (response to P1)
> HIGH SPEED WOULD MAKE IT REALLY LOOK SWEET.
> (response to P2)

In this example, Peter's message (P1) interrupts Ted's turn of listing systems where 'it' is operating. Then Peter's message (P2) arrives before Ted has replied to P1. As a result, Ted's last utterance consists of two moves: responses to two of Peter's utterances (P1 and P2).

Adjacency pairs are also often absent. In face-to-face and telephone conversations, questions are followed by answers, offers by acceptance (or refusal) and so on. Again because of the time delay, a question may not be answered immediately. And, the sender does not consider this rude; rather, she assumes the recipient is working on the problem or request and will reply when she has the needed information. While the norm for middle-class white interaction is flouted, such communication patterns are the norm in other cultural settings, such as among Warm Springs Indians of Central Oregon, described by Susan Urmstrom Philips (1983).

OPENINGS AND CLOSINGS

In CmC, openings and closings are optional. Users quite often launch straight into their request or content, without any of the usual conventional phatic communication, a characteristic of a conversation that focuses on transactions rather than interactions.

Again, it is the particular context of CmC that makes this possible – an interactive, written medium where the usual paralinguistic and non-linguistic cues are absent.

In other conversations, either the identity of the participants is known (because they can see each other) or the speaker self-identifies (e.g., the telephone caller). In CmC self-identification is optional. In most e-message and e-mail systems, the node and userid of the sender are supplied by the computer system. In addition, most e-mail users have an automatic header which gives their name such as in the earlier examples under e-mail). Even so, some people always end their e-mail with a sign-off, either of their name, or their first initial. It is as though the name impersonally supplied by the computer does not carry the same interpersonal value as the personal signing by the individual, a strategy similar to that used in typewriting and wordprocessing of letters – although we may type our name, we also sign it by hand. In e-messages, people only self-identify if they would not be recognized – if, for example, they are using another person's userid. In bulletin boards, participants often take on pseudonyms and deliberately remain anonymous.

A summons is used in communication to get the attention of the person we want to talk to. In face-to-face conversations this mainly occurs when we call to someone who is not close enough to begin talking to or is busy doing something else. With the telephone, the summons is the ringing. Because CmC is remote, summons is common. In e-messages, it often takes the form of sending a short e-message (e.g., 'hi,' 'you there?') to determine whether the recipient is available and willing to engage in an interactive conversation. Because this is an interactive mode of conversation, the sender needs to know if the recipient is available. Perhaps the recipient is at her terminal, but is busy with other work; or perhaps she has a colleague in the office with her and does not want to engage in what might be a sensitive conversation. In e-mail, the summons is the arrival of the mail. Because this is not an interactive mode and goes only to the recipient, there is no need for a linguistic summons to open the channels of communication. In this case, e-message conversations operate more like face-to-face and telephone conversations, while e-mail conversations operate more like regular mail.

In face-to-face and telephone conversations, participants greet each other and often name the addressee such as

S1: Hi, Sue. How are you?
S2: Oh, hi, Jim. Fine. How about you?

In e-messages, greetings and naming addressee rarely occur; in e-mail they may occur on first contact. Since the technology provides the name of the recipients and the sender has determined exactly who will receive the message, naming the addressee is redundant. And, the prologue seems to take the place of a greeting as well. When naming of addressee occurs, its use is usually marked. For example, if an e-mail message is addressed to several people, the sender may name one person and talk directly to that person (see the example below). Clearly this is not the whisper in computer conferences since all recipients read it. It is merely a time saver – the sender does not need to send separate e-mail to the individual.

> Gretings everyone! bet you thought I had died or something Iv'e been reading the analyses and I'm going to take a stab at my own. Before I start I want to say that I'm going to be making a copy of all of the assign.(#9) so I can go over them at home. Susan , I have to go over yours again because I think we have very similar written material and many of the same falacies apply. We will have to compare more in class.

Duranti (1986) found especially interesting usage of naming the addressee among his students. They did it when apologising or complaining to their professor – perhaps because of the unequal status between professor and student. But the particular ways students named their professor demonstrates the tension between power and solidarity. Many of the students used the professor's first name, which, in United States usage signals solidarity.

In face-to-face conversations, closing resembles a dance with several closing elements negotiated by the participants. In CmC it is more direct and often absent. E-message conversations are often suspended without any formal linguistic sign. The silence is interpreted as a closing, and is not considered rude. People know that systems fail, and other conversations take precedence. E-mail, too, may just have the signature or a brief terminal such as 'bye'.

MULTIPLE THREADS OF DISCOURSE

Another feature of CmC is that the number of content threads is greater with CmC than with face-to-face conversation. The latter is primarily sequential, constrained by the evanescent nature of speech. CmC, however, allows for and actually facilitates multiple discourse topics going on at the same time. Conversations become separated by other conversations on different topics. Many interactants find it difficult to follow which conversation some particular content is related to and so often request narrow topics for computer conferences. Or, moderators, seeing the development of another on-going topic, start a new conference on this topic.

Other users, suggesting rules of etiquette for CmC use (see pp. 88–89 for details) suggest each e-mail message or conference contribution should be on one topic only, in an attempt to maintain Grice's maxim of relevance. Still others have developed programs to ensure this unity of conversations, as we saw with The Coordinator in Chapter 3. While such activities may prevent confusion, they also deny one of CmC's advantages over face-to-face conversation – its very ability to have multiple content threads. The real question to address is how we can technically store and access such data. Currently, most people file their e-mail under topic, sender, or time. If they choose topic, they have a dilemma when e-mail comes with multiple content threads. If they choose sender or time, they do not have all e-mail on the one topic (and therefore part of the same conversation) in one file. What is needed for CmC to exploit its ability to have multiple topics is an efficient data storage and retrieval system – that is still to come.

Interpersonal relations

The context that has resulted in changes to language and the organization of conversations, has also contributed to differences in the way people interact via CmC. In particular, researchers have noted changes in the way users perceive themselves and their audience. Thus, we find evidence that the usual barriers to interaction are broken down, resulting in a more participatory but also less constrained interaction.

In established forms of communication, we know the conventions, whether they are conscious or not. In CmC, many of the cues for these conventions, such as paralinguistic and non-linguistic cues, are not visible. We may not know the name, let alone the status, of other participants; we can not see when someone disapproves of our statement; we can not be interrupted. Thus, as one e-mail user reported:

> Sometimes I think that electronic mail is more of an addiction for me than the computer is. I talk to people all over the country. When you

type mail into the computer you feel you can say anything . . . sometimes it gets pretty personal . . . The touch [of the computer] is very
sensitive . . . I would say that I have a perfect interface with the machine
– perfect for me. I feel totally telepathic with the computer. And it sort of
generalizes so that I feel telepathic with the people I am sending mail to.
I am glad I don't have to see them face to face. I wouldn't be as personal
about myself.

(Turkle 1984, p. 211)

People who normally feel pressured and threatened by face-to-
face interactions and who let others dominate the conversation can
have equal time. Usual turn-taking rules do not apply – men or
others with power will not dominate topics and interrupt. Using
body language such as eye contact to avoid passing turns or to
force a turn does not occur. There is no pressure to respond immediately (or at all). There are no norms about staying on topic. A
question asked one day may not be responded to for hours, days or
even weeks, without appearing rude. Because of the sense of autonomy, members contribute more equally to the conversation; one
person tends to dominate less; people do not defer to one person as
much; people change their minds and abandon previous positions.
As a result, they take longer to reach agreement; their final decisions are more extreme, involving more risk but are usually as
good as or slightly better than face-to-face group decisions; and the
participants believe more strongly in the rightness of their final
group decisions. But, these very advantages can cause computer
conferences to flounder and both researchers and participants call
for strong leadership for computer conferences to be successful.
Strong leaders can provide focus for discussion and also organize
the multiple discourse threads so prevalent in CmC. Of course,
while without strong leadership conferences are unsuccessful,
leadership itself does not guarantee success since others must contribute as well as read responses.

On the other hand, researchers and others have noted that
people, freed from the conventions of established communication,
may be more rude, profane and emotional, a phenomenon called
'flaming'. As one French Minitel user says

It made me think about language, about communication, and how to
seduce with words. On the Mintel, there is no voice, no perfumes, no
touch, no eyes. You can say what you want. You can lie.

(Reported in San José Mercury News, 4 October 1987, p. 6A)

Similarly, Hiltz and Turoff report of

> the most intimate of exchanges taking place between persons who have
> never met face-to-face and probably never will. Revelations about
> personal inadequacies, deviant preferences, past love affairs, and serious
> personal problems that the sender may have told no one else except
> his/her psychiatrist have passed through the EIES system.
>
> (Hiltz and Turoff 1978, p. 28)

Not all studies have found evidence of flaming and have found instead a more extensive use of politeness markers. The difference is largely because of the context of situation in which CmC takes place. In the settings with minimum flaming, the conversations have focused on transactions, that is, on conversation for action, more than on interaction. So, the medium is not the sole determiner of language use – other aspects of the context also affect the way people use language.

In reaction to uninhibited expression, many organizations and individuals have called for 'etiquette rules' (called netiquette) for CmC such as the following that Judith Windt wrote in 1983 (note that she does not differentiate among e-messages, e-mail, bulletin boards, and conferences):

- Try to keep in mind who you are sending the message to: Should you be flippant, business-like, breezy or to the point? Until you really become friendly with the person, it's safer to err on the side of formality.
- If the message is long or complicated, or if you want the person to comment on it, note in the message that a paper copy is to follow. Most people find it difficult to read from a computer terminal screen, and even fewer can edit someone else's material on a computer screen – copy editors excepted, of course.
- Follow up, or precede complicated or potentially ambiguous messages with a face-to-face meeting, or a phone call.
- Try to read and answer all your messages as soon as possible.
- Remember that the flesh-and-blood person standing in your office should come first, the caller on the telephone should come second, and the computer message should come last in the list of priorities. This means you should not keep swiveling away from the person in your office to answer each message that leaps onto your screen.
- Never try to weasel past another person's office visitor or telephone busy signals via computer messages.

- Send yourself a copy of the message you send someone else, especially if it requires a reply.
- Resist the temptation to read the messages on the screen of the person you are visiting.
- Learn to protect yourself from prying eyes . . . kill the message . . . if someone is approaching your work area.
- It's best not to use the computer for gossip.
- Electronic messages give us access to people we would not ordinarily have access to. Nevertheless don't send messages to the company president unless he or she asks you to.
- Control the need to 'flame out' over the system . . . Be courteous.
- Try not to make your messages so letter-perfect that the recipient will think you spend all your time carefully writing and editing messages. Let typos sneak in. The recipient feels less threatened that way.
- Finally, do make it a practice to send pleasant messages . . . praise for a job well done.

    (*San José Mercury News*, 30 November 1983, pp. 1D and 2D)

Since then, such lists have proliferated in many different domains. While most of the suggestions made in such advice lists do address serious concerns among CmC users, we must note that we do not have similar lists of rules for face-to-face or even telephone conversations – those conversations work through people applying unwritten norms that they learn as they negotiate with others while acquiring the language. Why then are we requiring written rules for CmC? I believe it is not only because it is a new medium, with as yet fluid conventions, but also because it is a written medium. We have hundreds of manuals for written English, from style books to books on how to write letters. Because we can be judged over time by our written texts, Western literate society is far more concerned about the written word than the spoken. Our laws of plagiarism and libel focus on what is written – on permanent records (although we do have copyright laws for tapes and disks, etc.). This question of ownership and responsibility will be taken up again in Chapter 6 in the discussion on wordprocessing, and again in Chapter 8 in the discussion of the public nature of communication.

How do people fit this new medium into their repertoire of means of interaction?

Although popular opinion claims that our children's reliance on computers (and especially computer games) is producing an illiterate generation, CmC actually *requires* literacy skills, as does most current interaction with computers. Since 'the technology of literacy, then, is a cultural form, a social product whose shape and influence depend on prior political and ideological factors' (Street 1984, p. 96), we must examine literacy practices over all media in order to determine where this medium of CmC fits.

In my eight-month study within IBM, I found that computer-mediated communication has become part of an expanded repertoire of literacy practices in industry. Workers move and choose among the range of available media: pen and ink, typewriter, telephone, computer and face-to-face. In other words, available media are options from which speakers choose (not necessarily consciously), in the same way that they make other linguistic choices. What motivates the choice of medium? Speakers move from one medium to another as the context of their interaction changes. The aspects of the context that result in medium choice form a complex, hierarchically organized taxonomy (see table below).

Taxonomy of Factors Contributing to Choice of Mode.
(Source: Murray 1991, p. 67.)

---

1. Field
    1.1 Topic
        • sensitive/open
        • simple/complex
    1.2 Organization of Topic
        • parallel threads
        • episodic threads
    1.3 Focus of Topic
        • on social cohesion
        • on action
        • unfocused
    1.4 Distance between Language and Activity
2 Speaker/Hearer
    2.1 Knowledge of Audience
        • who is potential audience
        • audience size

- conversational style
2.2 Role Relations
- power: institutional, personal, and expertise
- affect
- contact
3. Setting
3.1 Institutional Conventions
3.2 Space
- Distance Between Speaker and Hearer
  – available channels
  – interactivity
  – permanence
  – planning
- Availability
3.3 Time
- time zone
- time management
- physical constraints

To illustrate, I will describe two situations. People in my IBM study deal with sensitive messages by switching media. In one such case, I had asked several people at one particular research laboratory to participate in a questionnaire. Most were willing, but a couple had said they wanted management approval before they would agree to participate. I told John, my manager, and Stuart, my project manager, through e-mail before I went out of town for several days. On my return I read e-mail from Stuart telling me he had not received objections from anyone else concerning the questionnaire. Knowing I had just returned, John began an e-message dialogue that went as follows:

J1: WELCOME BACK!
J2: GIME A SHOUT WHEN YOU HAVE SOME TIME . . . I HAVE SOME INTERESTING FEEDBACK TO SHARE WITH YOU. . .
J3: FROM OUR NEAT-O 'FRIENDS'.
M1: yep, right now – was just sending a note to stuart on same subject.
J4: OK, I'LL HEAD DOWN TO YOUR OFFICE.

John chose to continue with face-to-face communication because the topic was extremely sensitive, involving reporting what he had been told by a third party whom he did not want to name or implicate. Further, he wanted to be sure that I fully understood the delicacy of the situation. He told me he chose face-to-face so it could not be overheard and so all the physical (paralinguistic) cues would be available for him to present his case and thereby ensure that I had interpreted the information as he intended. Thus, the nature of the topic often constrains the choice of medium.

Another aspect of the context that constrains choice of medium is interpersonal relations. The need to use paralinguistic and non-linguistic cues that are missing in written forms constrains the use of CmC (and other written forms). This restriction plays an especially important role in people's use of medium since CmC is such a new medium that conventions for establishing voice are still being established (despite the occasional use of icons), unlike other established written media (such as business letters), where genre conventions are well-established and known by the speech community. In one such situation, Peter switched medium since there was a possible confusion between institutional power and personal power. Peter and his system programmer, Ted, are personal friends. They became involved in a lengthy computer conversation disagreement over manuals to help users. Rather than continue with e-messages, Peter sent Ted an e-message that said:

> please call – we've *got* to discuss. call me when you get to work.

Earlier in the same interaction, Peter questioned why Ted had installed a new system before completely debugging it. He expressed annoyance first, by typing 'humpf' and later, by typing 'sigh', when Ted indicated that he had not installed all the necessary access codes. After more CmC discussion that did not resolve the problems, Peter asked Ted to call. Later in an interview, he claimed that had he continued to press for more documentation through e-messages, Ted might have thought he was enforcing his institutional role of manager, which he did not want to do. He felt that in a telephone call he could more easily establish equal role status, especially through the use of intonation and stress.

From these examples we can see that, although the medium of communication is a feature of the context, it is also determined by the interplay of other aspects of the context. In other words, medium represents linguistic choices, choices made because of the characteristics of the particular context in which the interaction takes place. This leads to a rethinking of orality and literacy. Orality and literacy are not dichotomous, nor do they represent ends of a continuum along which various types of literate and oral modes can be placed as a result of their specific characteristics. E-message and e-mail, although in written form, often share characteristics claimed to identify oral language, such as fragmentation, and personal involvement; however, e-mail can share characteristics of written language. Moreover, people move among media even within the same interaction.

Thus, the appearance of characteristics such as integration, personal involvement, etc. are primarily the result of the specific context, not of whether the discourse is written or oral. If the role relation is one of high effect, high contact, and low power, we would expect greater use of the characteristics Chafe (1982) has identified with personal involvement – use of personal pronouns and hedging – whether the discourse is written or oral. If the focus is on action, we would expect more active voice and direct quotations.

In addition, the choice of medium is itself an indicator of context through association. Thus, when one participant medium-switches, the switch is an indicator to the recipient that there is likely to be some associated change in topic, speaker/hearer, and/or setting.

Thus, any theory of literacy must account for the relationship between oral and written language and the context. Recurring contexts result in institutionalized choices of media for varying speech communities at various times. Thus, within the IBM community I studied, contracts, although constructed and drafted through e-mail, always take their final form in print.

While these IBM workers, and many others have incorporated CmC into their repertoire, in general, the public is only just beginning to accept this medium, even though it has been around for two decades. Bulletin boards have become most popular, but not e-messages, e-mail, and computer conferences only marginally. CmC systems are mostly accepted by users who have some previous experience with computers, have their own personal computer or computer terminal, and are geographically dispersed, most of which are not the case for the general public. Yet, the need for almost instantaneous communication is great. They have instead, turned to a newer technology–fax–because it is simple to use, being a simple extension of the photocopy machine and telephone. Another factor may be the metaphors of mail and conference we use to describe these CmC uses. As long as we think of e-mail as mail, we ignore its use as a transmitter of documents. So, too, as long as we think of computer conferences, we ignore the complex genres available through this mode.

Fax is fast becoming the preferred form for electronic transmission among businesses and between the general public and small and large businesses and government offices. Australia, for example, with a population of only 18 million, had 220,000 faxes installed in 1989 and signed an agreement with France and Canada to provide fax facilities on 330 airlines, including Qantas (Australia's national airline). In universities and within many companies and government agencies, however, e-mail is preferred. When I meet new colleagues at a conference, for example, instead of asking for my street address, they ask for my BITNET address.

Superficially, at least, it is difficult to explain the sudden, enormous popularity of fax. On the face of it, fax is inferior to e-mail. Granted that fax can transmit graphics, including letter heads, drawings, even crudely rendered photographs and (perhaps most significantly) signatures. Yet, e-mail can do the same kind of things; the more sophisticated wordprocessors, and certainly the popular desktop publishing systems, can render all these non-textual elements and communications programs (and e-mail systems) can transmit them. Electronic signature schemes have been proposed, most of which have the added advantage of providing secure transmission through encryption.

Fax machines and personal computers are comparably priced and a PC is considerably more versatile since it can be used for many other purposes in the office and home. Still, neither is unobtainably priced and it is no surprise to find both machines in a household of moderate professional means.

Bit-for-bit, fax transmission is generally more expensive than e-mail, certainly over long distances and for text (which is, by far, the most common purpose for both systems). E-mail uses high bandwidth (much cheaper per bit) transmission facilities, can operate at non-peak periods (further reducing cost) and can utilize very sophisticated data compression and error detection/correction techniques to greatly reduce the amount of data actually transmitted (again reducing cost).

Fax delivers a printed image, on paper which is, again, redundant and wasteful when text and information transfer are the desired object. Fax material is not easily manipulated on the receiving end since most faxes produce only paper output, not online output. Thus, when a colleague and I are writing a joint paper, if I send a copy to her via fax, she can not manipulate my actual text. She receives a hard copy that she can manually edit and then return with the handwritten additions. Fax recipients go to great lengths in order to have a manipulable text. I have heard of people receiving fax on paper, which they then input to a computer in digital form using a scanner followed by a conversion (using a program) into text form (a not very efficient process since there are fax cards for PCs which will, at least, receive the already digitized fax format). The 'back translation' process from 'bit-scanned' format back to text has limited effectiveness and considerable editing and re-creation of text is needed. The thought of a world using PCs with elaborate desktop publishing programs to produce beautifully formatted text/graphics images on a laser printer, which are then transmitted to the recipient using fax, who then converts it all back to desktop publisher format using a scanner, re-creates the text, edits it and sends it back and/or otherwise replies the same way – is simply mind boggling! Despite its superior capability of transmitting graphics, fax is not effective for the transmission of binary data (including encrypted data which are randomized bit strings) and common binarized formats like spreadsheets, databases, word-processor files, etc.

Fax transmission is essentially synchronous, lacking the store and forward conveniences of e-mail. With fax, a point-to-point phone call must be made, completed, and held for the duration of the transmission. Line errors, noise and broken connections require a complete re-dial, connect, transmission sequence. Busy lines, and so forth, impede the process and introduce errors.

Why then the overwhelming popularity of fax over e-mail for public communications (as opposed to corporate, proprietary, academic, or intra-government systems) – even at greatly increased cost (dollars and convenience)? Fax owners are numbered in the tens of millions. Public e-mail users are still relatively rare although there are many millions of PC owners. The answer is simple – an easy to use machine and a universal standard for the fax user; a complex machine system and a tower of babel for the e-mail subscriber.

For fax, all you need is a fax machine and a telephone. Dial the number (we all know how to do that), put the paper in the machine and it is all done. Never mind that this is not quite exactly what we want done. But, it is better than the alternative (an envelope, stamp, trip to the post box and several days of postal delays). And, it can be sent anywhere there is telephone service.

Despite its success in closed environments, practical e-mail for the public does not exist. E-mail suffers from a multitude of different standards established by many different companies. In most cases, e-mail utilities can not talk to each other, making efficient interaction across states, countries, and organizations difficult and most often, impossible. The problem of standards is solved within the academic community since computer scientists and programmers at various gateways have written programs that allow different systems to interface with each other. However, even so, there is no single interface even in BITNET and if I move from campus to campus, I have to learn a new protocol for accessing BITNET. With e-mail the received text is in electronic form and can therefore be manipulated. If a colleague and I are writing a paper together, she can receive my copy, add, edit, and revise my document online and return the revised version to me and I can then revise, etc. and so on. However, this potential is not realized by many interactants because of the lack of standards in wordprocessing and e-mail conversion and transmission codes. If I am writing my document with a wordprocessor, I will have to convert the document to ASCII format before I send it. My colleague then receives a copy that does not have formatting controls, but does have carriage returns. For her to manipulate my text using her wordprocessor, she has to bring the ASCII file into her wordprocessor and then 'massage' it to remove and add format controls. This is not the case with most LANs or within companies that have their own internal standard. Thus, within IBM, for example, employees can send electronic text around the world, where it can be revised by any number of colleagues and returned – all without any conversions. Were this the case for the general public, e-mail may have become more popular by now.

An even more overwhelming reason for the lack of popularity of e-mail compared with fax is that e-mail is not as simple as fax, requiring some computer literacy and a number of steps: logging on to one's own computer or terminal; loading a communications package; signing on to the e-mail system with name and password (and remembering userid and password!); often dealing with a difficult editor to write the document; using a command to send the document. Identification codes are typically obtuse in e-mail systems.

While CmC is only just catching the general public's attention, it has proliferated in many other domains, adding to people's communication repertoire. Bulletin boards, however, have become like the village square, a site for talk and discussion. What is clear about all these new communications media, is that

> Current transformations in telecommunications – like earlier transforma-
> tions in speech, writing, and printing – will not replace earlier media.
> Reading and writing did not eliminate speech. Nor did television rele-
> gate the printing press or the radio to the scrap heap. Each new
> technology added to the communication options. The same will be true
> today. . . The more complicated truth is that the future menu of media
> options will be enlarged.
>
> (Abramson et al. 1988, pp. 32–3)

FOR DISCUSSION

1. This chapter has posited reasons why fax has become more popular than e-mail. What technical and societal changes need to
   take place for e-mail to be more widely used?
2. This chapter has shown how differently people use language in
   CmC than in other communication media. As CmC becomes
   more widely used, in what ways do you think some of these
   more extreme changes (e.g., flaming) will tend towards a middle
   ground. How might the language look?
3. How important is it for you to know background information
   about your interactants? Would you feel comfortable using an
   anonymous bulletin board? Or carrying on a long e-mail conversation with someone you do not know?
4. This chapter has shown the trend to supervise CmC. In what
   ways is CmC like print and broadcasting and so under the controls of those media? In what ways is it more like the telephone,
   without such controls? What controls do you think are necessary? Why? (Note: this issue will be raised again in Chapter 8;
   but these questions will act as advance organizers for that discussion.)

FOR ACTION

1. Use both a fax machine and e-mail. What differences did you
   notice—in ease of use, convenience, technical capabilities?
2. Gain access to a bulletin board (or interview someone who uses
   one). What is the main purpose of the bulletin board? What

controls are there? Can you 'whisper?' Who has access to the bulletin board?

3. Examine a printout from a bulletin board, computer conference, or e-mail conversation. Compare the use of language with that described here – e.g., Is it a simplified register? Is there flaming? How is the conversation organized?

FURTHER READING

Hiltz and Turoff (1978) is the seminal study of computer conferencing. Kerr and Hiltz (1982) summarize research on computer conferences. Murray (1991) gives a thorough linguistic analysis of CmC. *Written Communication*, January 1991 is devoted to CmC. Sproull and Kiesler (1986) examine the social effects of networking in organizations.

SIX

The computer as text processor

> Michelle works for a law firm as a paralegal secretary. She prides
> herself on her fast and accurate work, and sees the firm's recently
> installed word-processing system as a threat to her arduously acquired
> skills. Her terminal sits at her desk, unused and ignored, as she
> continues to use her electric typewriter. She has used the word
> processor only when her employer insists.
>
> (Brod 1984, p. 37)

For Michelle, the computer as text processor is a threat to both her
self-esteem and, she believes, her livelihood. She is one example of
workers who would need to re-tool and reassess their own definition of self in order to accommodate to the new technology.

Wherever information must be stored, retrieved, selected and
modified, wordprocessing has become the most common process
for information workers. Indeed, according to Dennis Longley and
Michael Shain,

> Word processing systems and applications represent the vanguard of
> the technological assault on the office. Wherever introduced they are
> likely over time to produce no less dramatic changes in working
> practices, individual responsibilities and interpersonnel [sic]
> relationships than the advent of automation did on the factory floor.
>
> (Longley and Shain 1984, p. 99)

This chapter will therefore discuss the quality and quantity of the
information work produced through wordprocessing. What is the
impact of wordprocessing on human thought processes? On the
relationships between text, writer and audience? And on the nature
of text itself?

As we saw in Chapter 2, our traditional notions about what constitutes 'text' and what constitutes 'oral language' have been very
clear: text is fixed and permanent while oral language is evanescent; meaning and authority are lodged in text, but not in oral

language. As a result of its permanence and authority, writing is the suitable vehicle for rational, critical thinking. It is analytical and sequential, and it is integrated. Oral language, on the other hand, is personal and emotional, formulaic, context-bound and fragmented. Such descriptions are inadequate when we consider the construction of texts through the medium of the computer and lead us to rethink our definitions of both orality and literacy. Even the more recent conceptualization of literacy and orality as forming a continuum is inadequate for discussing computer texts. While a casual dinner party conversation and an academic paper may represent either end of such a continuum, with computer texts we find written texts that are like casual conversation.

Are the texts we create online ever truly permanent? Do they have embodied in them the authority of the printed word? These questions will be answered by examining four major aspects of text as in the diagram below:

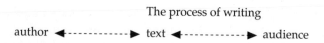

The texts discussed are those that are produced to help carry out the tasks of our working, intellectual or private lives. Most of us are by now familiar with wordprocessing and some of us may be familiar with text formatters. Text formatters differ from word processors in that the writer *explicitly* inserts control commands to define the appearance of the final document while typing the document. These commands do not take effect until the document is formatted when printed to the screen or to paper as a later (separate) step. The essence of wordprocessors, on the other hand, is what you see on the screen while typing the text, is what you get on the page when the text is printed (within the technical limitations of the display screen and printer to represent each other.) This feature of *what you see is what you get* is often referred to as WYSIWYG. For the purposes of the discussion here, the differences are not significant.

THE PROCESS OF WRITING ELECTRONIC TEXT

Eugenia, a lawyer, was writing up a brief that included a statement of her position on a case, possible rebuttals, and citations of prior cases on the issue. In preparing the brief, she followed a method used by many report writers in school, business, law, and other professions. After reading, thinking, and talking about the case, Eugenia outlined the major points of her argument. She created a text on the computer, including a list of the major points, which she reordered several times with the sentence-move commands on her word processor. She then wrote the argument for the point she felt was the strongest. She decided to present this point last, but she wrote it out first and then inserted the other points as she completed them. As her legal assistants found the exact citations for relevant court cases, she transferred the necessary facts from the citations into the appropriate places in her text. The document grew in stages, and she was always able to consider it from clearly typed and formatted pages. When the document was almost complete, Eugenia decided to move the last point to the beginning because it was the strongest opener.

(Daiute 1985, p. 38)

The wordprocessor allowed this writer to build her text around her initial set of notes, while at the same time providing clear, printed text, freeing her from the difficulties of reading hand-written notes, of finding the pieces of paper to cut and paste. The writing process for Eugenia was aided by the computer as text processor.

Most novice users of wordprocessing programs first express a feeling of liberation, of freedom. They can move text around, they can change, add, delete, underline, indent, all with a few key-strokes. They are impressed by the speed and quantity of wordprocessed text, by the freedom to continue writing without interruption. With a wordprocessor, while writing, they do not have to use any keys other than those for text; they can insert head-ers, underlines, check for typos, and so on later in the process. The wordprocessor frees us to concentrate on our ideas rather than on rhetoric, syntax, or punctuation. When changes are made, they appear instantaneously on the screen. Text is no longer rigid and fixed; it is infinitely malleable and changeable. Once users of word-processors have moved beyond the novice stage, they choose (perhaps) to write macros, short programs that customize their wordprocessing program for their own particular needs. For exam-ple, if I always indent a new paragraph five spaces and leave a line between it and the previous paragraph, I can define a key that will end the current line, move forward one line and indent five spaces on the subsequent line. Without this macro, I would need to hit enter twice and then indent. Even more complex manipulations can be customized, such as moving all footnotes at the bottom of pages to a notes section at the end of the chapter or paper. Such macros are indispensable for the scholar who submits work to journals that require different formatting styles. Wordprocessors themselves are, in a sense, a series of such macros, but ones designed for universal appeal. One wordprocessor, *Note Bene*, was designed by scholars for other scholars and so makes changing from one pre-defined style (e.g., *Chicago Manual of Style*) to another (e.g., *American Psychological Associations Manual*) very easy. Since then, several other companies have produced add-on software to standard wordprocessing packages that perform the same function. I used one such package to develop the reference list for this book.

Another aspect of computer writing is the replacement of the physical act of handwriting by the act of typing. While some scholars, such as the philosopher Heim (1987), decry this shift away from the personal, inscribed text to mechanized transcription, others have demonstrated how this freedom from scribal labour motivates children (see, for example, Daiute 1985 and Greenfield 1984), dyslexics (see, for example, Arkin and Gallagher 1984), and others. Part of the success of the IBM early literacy project, *Writing to Read*, results from kindergarten children being able to type in what they say while they are still too young to have the psycho-motor control necessary for handwriting. Handwriting requires much greater coordination and control than keyboarding, as we can see by the number of children and teenagers who, while semi-literate, play video games and computer games with ease.

The distance between handwriting and computer writing is even greater in non-alphabetical languages having characters and syllabaries. If we accept there is some physical difference between the inscribing of alphabetic writing and keyboarding, we can imagine the even greater difference between the calligraphy of characters and keyboarding. This difference is accentuated since any character-language keyboarding is always only an approximation or coding of the actual characters, done to achieve greater simplicity of both keyboards and input. The Japanese face the biggest problem since their writing system is a mélange of borrowed Chinese characters (kanji), indigenous syllabaries (kana), and the roman alphabet (romaji), and, unlike the Chinese and Koreans, they are unwilling to abandon this complex system for the sake of simplified input and output. Not only is the input of such a writing system virtually impossible, because of its multiple readings of kanji and the numerous inconsistencies of kana and romaji, but the machine recognition of such a system and the coding of characters are, according to Unger (1987), impossible. Unger claims that the premise on which the Japanese Fifth Generation Project is built, that artificial intelligence will provide the breakthrough for using the Japanese writing system, is fallacious. I will discuss this claim in detail in the following chapter when I look at artificial intelligence. For now, I will focus on the problems inherent in the Japanese writing system as they relate to text processing. Since the Japanese have insisted upon using their entire range of writing systems, many Japanese companies have developed Japanese-language word-processors. Because of the complexity of the script(s), these are neither easy to use nor fast. Further, their consistent use causes people to forget the very kanji the advocates of Japanese-language input seek to promote!

Another aspect of the process of electronic writing is the use of acronyms and abbreviations. Many of these are already provided by the computer operating system or the wordprocessor. So, we get used to 'PgDn' to stand for advancing the screen or page, for example. Because of space limitations for file names, we quickly develop systematic abbreviations for file naming. If we do not, chaos ensues and we find we are unable to retrieve files without sorting through everything. Even with the icon-driven Macintosh, the user has to name files.

Several programs are on the market for supporting the writing process. These are either prewriting tools, revising tools, or both. The prewriting tools are designed to aid invention, to help writers get ideas and play with their ideas. They range from formally structured outline programs to games simulating the rollers on a slot machine. Outline programs can be quite freeform, unlike the rigid outlines we are used to in pen-and-ink media. Outliners enable writers to see their text in a number of different ways. The text becomes a scratch pad for moving and changing headings and subheadings, for hiding or displaying the text behind the headings, for showing hierarchical relationships between parts of text. These outliners allow writers to play, to freely create new associations, to experiment. Writers can then try to structure these creative ideas, using their analytical skills rather than their creative juices. Even without such prewriting tools, invention is enhanced since we can concentrate on ideas rather than form. But, they can have disadvantages. Novices may focus on playing with the arrangement of ideas rather than on the ideas themselves (Dobrin 1987). They do not necessarily make writing from an outline any easier; the writer still has to translate the outline into text. And, writers who discover meaning through writing rather than outlining find no advantage in idea processors.

In instructional settings, to help liberate learners from attention to form, composition instructors often get students to 'free write', that is, write either on any topic or the topic of their essay for a set time without lifting the pen from the paper. If the student wants to pause, she is instructed to write down what she is actually thinking, even if it is only 'I can't think of anything to write. I can't think of anything to write.' With the computer, the writer can be completely freed from attention to form by using invisible writing as a form of freewriting. With invisible writing, the instructions are the same, but the writer turns off the computer screen. Thus, she cannot see what she has written and so has nothing to distract her from her ideas.

Writing with a computer increases the quantity of text; but what about the quality? Can that also be automated? Several revising tools are on the market, but, as we shall see, they focus more on surface level editing than on revising text for organization and ideas. These editing tools (I will call them editing rather than revising tools since they do not really aid major revision) include style analysers (including some attention to grammar), spell checkers, a thesaurus, and tools that reorganize the text.

Style analysers include Writer's Workbench and RightWriter, which count the number of words per sentence, the lengths of words, the number of passives and nominalizations, and the readability level. Writer's Workbench was developed at Bell Laboratories in response to criticism of unreadable computer documentation. Developed as an in-house tool so that technical writers could edit their own documents, it is now used in many companies and colleges. RightWriter was primarily designed for business and technical writing, but does allow the user to choose from a number of styles: general business, technical reports and articles, proposals, manuals and fiction. In all such style analysers, the writer receives a report that gives the average of each category and can then decide whether he wants to make some alterations to the text. Since linguists do not have a complete grammar of English (or any other language for that matter), these programs focus on the sort of principles of clear, direct writing that printed handbooks extol: use active rather than passive voice; avoid jargon and clichés; avoid long sentences; do not use too many descriptive adverbs and adjectives and so on. When I ran the previous paragraph through one of these style checkers, I was informed that the readability index was 12.55, that is, readers would need a 13th grade (first year of college) level of education to be able to read it since the writing is 'complex and may be difficult to read'. This conclusion was based largely on the use of passive voice in the second sentence and the length of the last two sentences.

It is fairly easy to trick such programs into identifying correct language as incorrect and vice versa. One such program, for example, will highlight 'It was red' as a passive. Evidently the rule in the program identifies passives as 'is/was/are/were + -ed'. A colleague at San Francisco State University, Richard Sammons, wrote the following incoherent text, which I also ran through one of these programs, with interesting results.

GRAMMAR, PUNCTUATION, STYLE: TEST PASSAGE

Grammar checkers promise to help we write good. Does they? His eyes are as blue as a Scandinavian. Her Majesty the Queen of England is a nifty chick. Having never been in a large city before, the noise and confusion seemed rather terrifying. About sentence fragments. Ten chairs was in the room, and John gave it to I. Uncle Henry might have given me a birthday present if I had not throw a baseball through his window. Its nice to be back. San Franciscans enjoy better shopping facilities. San Spade turned Brigid into the police. A automobile is outside. I gave Fred a 'F' in the course.

The analysis includes in-text prompts that can be viewed interactively on the screen, as shown below.

GRAMMAR, PUNCTUATION, STYLE: TEST PASSAGE

Grammar checkers promise to help we write good. Does they? His eyes are as blue as a Scandinavian. Her Majesty the Queen of England is a nifty<<*_U1. **COLLOQUIAL: nifty** *>> chick<<*_U1. **COLLOQUIAL: chick** *>>. Having never been in a large city before, the noise and confusion seemed rather terrifying.<<*_**S11. IS SENTENCE TOO NEGATIVE?** *>> About sentence fragments. Ten chairs was<<*_**G1. DO SUBJECT AND VERB AGREE IN NUMBER?** *>> in the room, and John gave it to I. Uncle Henry might have given me a birthday present if I had not throw a baseball through his window.<<*_**G3. SPLIT INTO 2 SENTENCES?** *>><<*_**S3. LONG SENTENCE: 31 WORDS** *>> Its nice to be back. San Franciscans enjoy better shopping facilities. San Spade turned Brigid into the police. A<<*_G6. **REPLACE A BY AN** *>> automobile is outside. I gave Fred a 'F' in the course.

The program also provides a summary, which is reproduced below. The first section, which gives the name of the original file I wanted analysed (test2.rw) and the name of the marked-up file (test2.out), summarizes a variety of statistics the program produces. The readability index is based largely on the number of words per sentence and the number of syllables per word. The actual numbers can be requested in the summary, but I did not use this feature when I ran the analysis. Unlike my paragraph above, Sammons' paragraph requires only a grade 5 education level of its readers. The strength index is based on active vs. passive; simple vs. complex clause and sentence structure; simple vocabulary (free of slang, jargon and clichés); and positive language. My paragraph scored only 0.23 on the strength index, whereas Sammons' paragraph rated 0.71, indicating that mine should be made more direct. The descriptive index, based on the frequency of adjectives and adverbs, showed both paragraphs to be within the normal range. Neither had jargon or sentence structure recommendations, despite the Sammons' paragraph having the technical term, 'sentence fragment' and a verbless sentence. The words to review section identifies a number of different classes of words a writer may wish to avoid (such as jargon, colloquial, etc.). The majority in Sammons' summary fall under the general type 'reader may not understand', which is of little help to the writer, especially since it includes 'San Franciscans' and 'Scandinavians'.

What is interesting about this analysis is that it fails to identify a number of surface errors usually considered more serious than 'confusion'. It does not differentiate between adjectives and adverbs ('good' in sentence 1); it does not identify the lack of subject-verb agreement in sentence 2 or in sentence 6; it does not identify the sentence fragment (sentence 5); and so on. Even more importantly, the program does not check for cohesion and coherence. Admittedly, the user's manual does say that garbage can appear to be good writing; yet, the program is sold as 'The intelligent grammar, style, usage, and punctuation checker.'

<<** SUMMARY **>>

Overall critique for: test2.rw
Output document name: test2.OUT

READABILITY INDEX: 5.33

4th   6th   8th 10th 12th 14th
|****|*| | | | | | | | |
SIMPLE | —— GOOD —— | COMPLEX
Readers need a 5th grade level of education.

STRENGTH INDEX: 0.71

0.0   0.5   1.0
| **** | **** | **** | **** | **** | **** | **** | | | |
WEAK   STRONG
The strength of delivery is good, but can be improved.

DESCRIPTIVE INDEX: 0.33

0.1   0.5   0.9 1.1
| **** | **** | | | | | | | |
TERSE |— NORMAL— | WORDY
The use of adjectives and adverbs is normal.

JARGON INDEX: 0.00

SENTENCE STRUCTURE RECOMMENDATIONS:
15. No Recommendations.

   << WORDS TO REVIEW >>
Review this list for negative words (N), jargon (J),
colloquial words (C), misused words (M), misspellings (?),
or words which your reader may not understand (?).

I.(?) 1	brigid(?) 1
chick(C) 1	confusion(N) 1
fragments(?) 1	franciscans(?) 1
never(N) 1	nifty(C) 1
not(N) 1	scandinavian(?) 1
terrifying(N) 1	

   << END OF WORDS TO REVIEW LIST >>
   <<** END OF SUMMARY **>>

Included in the summary are numerous comparison analyses
that graphically show the writer how her text compares with the
Gettysburg Address, a Hemingway short story, and a life insurance
policy using criteria such as readability, number of words per sentence, number of letters per word, percentage of sentences in

passive voice, and prepositions as a percentage of all words. I have reproduced only one of these comparisons in the table below, that of grade level readability, which shows that 5th graders can read Sammons' test paragraph and a Hemingway short story, while only those with at least a 12th grade education can read the Gettysburg Address and a life insurance policy. The choice of text for comparisons is especially interesting since the Gettysburg Address was intended to be heard, not read, and Hemingway deliberately chose a direct, simple sentence style, even for mature and complex ideas. (I wonder what Hemingway and Lincoln would think of these analyses of their language?)

Comparison analysis	Readability grade level (Flesch-Kincaid method)		
Grade School 3 4 5 6 7 8	High School 9 10 11 12	College Fr So Jr Sr	Graduate School +1 +2 +3 +4 PhD

test2..rw

Gettysburg Address

Hemingway short story

Life insurance policy

While it is easy to make fun of such programs, they have been successfully adopted both in industry and colleges as editing tools. However, users must be aware that their 'advice' is neither infallible nor binding. The final choice lies with the writer. With novice writers in schools, this presents a problem since they do not have the expertise to decide when they should follow the program's advice and when they should not. Even more important, who is the arbiter of style? Who writes the program and makes the decision that 'confusion' is negative or that active voice is stronger than passive? While we are all familiar with various style manuals such as those produced by professional organizations or those used in college composition classes, the advice is of quite a different order – the writer must identify possible problems in writing and use the style manual for advice. The computer style checkers give the illusion of an informed person critiquing your paper. What is entirely missing is whether the text is in fact appropriate for its audience and purpose. A scientist describing a process may indeed want to use passive; a writer discussing Rajiv Ghandhi's assassination may want to say it caused confusion in India.

Similarly, with spell checkers, the writer is usually given a list of options for the incorrectly spelled word. The writer has to decide which option to choose. The better spell checkers recognize typographic as well as spelling errors. For example, since 'a' and 's' appear side-by-side on the keyboard and I am not a touch typist, I often hit one key when I intend the other. So, when I type 'snd' for 'and', the spell checker that comes packaged with my word processor includes both 'send' and 'and' among the many options. What no spell checker does is to recognize homophones or misspellings that are actual words. When I wrote my dissertation, I typed 'Tome Zone' instead of 'Time Zone' as a heading under which I was discussing the advantages of e-mail when people live and work in different time zones. It took a real person (a member of my committee, Terry Winograd) to notice this error. He wrote in the margin beside the words 'Is this the place all dissertations go to haunt professors?' Since then I have been much more conscientious in proofreading my texts myself and not just relying on spell checkers. I wonder how much time and effort the spell checker really saves and whether the result is significantly better.

Some revising tools do attempt to deal with organization and ideas. Writer's Helper Stage II, for example, displays only the first sentence of each paragraph so the writer can see if the ideas move clearly from paragraph to paragraph. Or it displays first and last sentences in each paragraph so the writer can determine whether she wandered afar in the paragraph.

Composition scholars in particular have studied the effects of prewriting revising and wordprocessing tools on the writing process. All the research agrees that both novice and expert writers produce more text when using a computer. In one such study (see Greenfield 1984), the researchers compared the writing of third/fourth graders writing with and without wordprocessors over a four-month period. The children using the wordprocessor increased the number of words in their essays by 64 per cent while the other class showed no increase. But, what about the quality of the writing? The research results are mixed. This same study of third/fourth graders showed an increase in quality, measured on a five-point scale, from 2.0 to 3.09 for those writing with computers and no increase for the control group. Some experimental studies have shown no overall difference in writing proficiency between pen and ink and computer writers (see, for example, Teichman and Poris 1989; Cross 1990). Others have shown that using computers to write has helped students develop a repertoire of revising strategies, helping them move beyond the novice stage (see, for example, Kelly and Raleigh 1990). Yet other research has shown that experienced writers do more higher level revising (see, for example, Case 1985), while weaker writers do more surface level editing than when they write without computers (see, for example, Collier 1983, Daiute 1986, and Harris 1985). These inexperienced writers make numerous changes, but primarily at the surface level; they do not revise for organization and ideas. Writers who do not like to revise are not necessarily encouraged to do so using a computer unless guided by an instructor. The more Beethovian writers, who develop their ideas as they compose, feel restricted by the wordprocessor, while the Mozartians, who compose in their heads first, find the wordprocessor suits their style. Burns and Culp (1980), however, found that guided questioning dialogues helped students articulate and refine their ideas, and focus more on point of view than on content in the invention stage of composing. One of the difficulties of the research is the novelty of the computer. It has not been possible to develop a research design that can separate out the computer as 'fun', new technology from its revising and editing functions. Further, no research has been done with experienced users of wordprocessors, comparing those who are proficient writers and those who are not. In addition, most research has had writers move from hard copy drafts to soft copy, creating an environment in which the computer is a typewriter rather than a tool for the process of writing. James Catano (1985), in examining the writing process of two professional writers, shows that for these writers, text is fluid:

> not simply [as] a series of words proceeding from page one to the end but as a gathered body of material that is constantly being expanded . . . with items being collected and stored, altered and rejected at all stages of the writing. The whole collection of materials exists as a unit, but one

that undergoes constant change and manipulation, that is, constant
revision.

(Catano 1985, p. 310)

In fact, both writers begin writing before they have any firm
notions of where their writing will go. Because of the malleability
of electronic text, they begin writing where they once listed,
free-wrote or clustered in hard copy. The new technology allows
these two professional writers to write recursively with ease; they
are adapting an already successful process of writing to the technology. But what of less skilful writers? Does the fact of using a
computer automatically lead them to a more successful process? It
seems not.

Grow (1988), for example, has shown that the writing of professionals who compose with computers but are not 'writers', rather
being professionals whose work requires them to write, exhibits a
number of problems either caused by, or accentuated by the computer. They fall into the editing trap, using multiple editing as a
substitute for rethinking the entire draft. They change surface
errors such as spelling, punctuation, or syntax, but fail to see that
the entire piece is disorganized or lacks supporting detail. Since collaboration is simplified by wordprocessing, a text may have many
authors, each exhibiting his or her own voice and style so that the
text becomes a collage rather than an integrated whole. Since many
writers have already written many reports or papers, they recycle
their own chunks of text, what Grow calls a 'clumsy kind of self-
plagiarism', even if the conventions, voice, or purpose of the new
text is different. The liberation of writers using a wordprocessor can
lead to prolific writing, the saying of the same thing in many different ways, or to terse, cryptic writing. Another feature of poor
professional writers Grow has observed has also been noted by
Diane Balestri (1988) at Princeton University: clean, formatted hard
copy is confused with well-written completed copy. We look at the
printout. It looks so professional, with bold face, italics, underlin-
ing, no white-outs or crunched type. It must be perfect. It looks just
like a printed book. She recommends that writing instructors prohibit learners from printing out their texts until the final draft. She
suggests they use soft copy to get the feel of the fluidity and infinitely editable nature of computer text, that they write to the
screen, not the printer.

Since computer writing is so speedy and instantaneous, what
Heim (1987) calls the 'contemplative concentration' and 'inner

suggestibility' that printed text produces are abandoned for 'the active expectation of the not yet verbalized'. The moment of procreation may be emphasized over gestation. The heady flow of ideas substitutes for the development and organization of ideas.

Despite the possible problems inherent in writing to the printer, there are liberating advantages, as described by Tanya, one of the many people interviewed by Sherry Turkle (1984) for her groundbreaking ethnographic study, *The Second Self*.

> Tanya's fifth-grade school record looks bleak: it reports she can't spell, can't add or subtract, doesn't write. It gives no hint of what is most striking when you meet her. Tanya has a passionate interest in words and the music of speech. 'I go by the word of the Lord, the word of the Bible. If you have the deep down Holy Ghost and you are speaking in the tongue which God has spoke through you, you harken to the word.' As Tanya speaks, she wraps herself in a rich world of language. She speaks apocalypse, salvation, and sin. The school language of readers and workbooks and sample sentences cannot compete with Tanya's flowing, tumbling discourse. She says, 'school is not a good place for my kind of words'.
>
> (Turkle 1984, p. 122)
>
> . . .
>
> The computer offered her a product that 'looked so clean and neat' that it was unquestionably right, a feeling of rightness she had never known at school, where she was always painfully aware of her deficiencies, ashamed of them, and, above all, afraid of being discovered as being stupid.
>
> (Ibid., p.125)

The motivating power of the computer is the common thread throughout all the research on writing with computers. The challenge for educators in particular, is to harness the energy, enthusiasm, and change in attitude towards writing so that inexperienced writers discover and are led to the successful strategies of successful writers.

Probably even more important is the need to reassess the privileged status of print (that is, books, journals, etc.) among intellectuals and the educational establishment. Many of us raised with the medium of print being the standard for measuring all other media are threatened by (or at least uncomfortable with) the new media. In this, we are no different from Plato who feared writing would weaken the mind, or scholar-priests in the fifteenth century who saw the printing press as a threat to their scholarly work. By privileging one medium (print) over another, we may deny the Tanyas of our world access to education for, as Marshall McLuhan (1964) says, 'we have confused reason with [print] literacy, and rationalism with a single technology [print writing]'. This is especially the case in this transitional stage, when those in positions of authority have been raised in the print culture, while those whom we teach, employ, or govern, are being exposed to a variety of media. These young people may not develop skills specialized primarily for reading; they will have a more diverse range of skills and media on which to draw. Indeed, they need this more diverse range of skills. The language of technology is primarily non-verbal and imagistic, according to E.S. Ferguson (1977). Thus, those involved with technology need to think in terms of images; but our schools (even our engineering schools) educate students to use numbers and words rather than visual images. How then can these engineers deal with real machines and materials? How long will Michelle be able to hold down her job as a para-legal secretary if she continues to resist the wordprocessor? We need to accept that, '[p]roperly used, every medium, without exception, can provide opportunities for human learning and development. The task now is to find a niche for each medium' (Greenfield 1984, p. 7).

AUTHORSHIP OF ELECTRONIC TEXT

Three children are clustered around the computer. First, Adam helps Alex learn to use the word-processing program as Michael looks on. All three boys then progress from discussing the word-processing operations to collaborating on a history assignment. Together, they develop a piece about the Civil War – each boy adding details and arguing about whether the war did or did not help America. They expand the text as they relate through it. Sometimes, they respond to one another by changing the text, rather than by talking. The collective work emerges with no handwriting differences to identify individual writers. The children even change one another's sentences slightly, so that few sentences remain that were written by an individual author.
(Daiute 1985, p. 27)

Carl, a business consultant who does a great deal of writing, began working with an outside typist last year. He would drive the three miles to her house to pick up material that she typed, and they would always sit and talk. Often she would give him ideas or make suggestions. Carl recalls, 'She would say, "You missed a point" or "This isn't very clear. . ." One day a few months ago, she called and said, "You don't have to come over here anymore. I'm getting an Apple and a modem. You use yours and send me stuff by phone." I actually felt distressed. There isn't the same back-and-forth anymore.'

(Brod 1984, p. 81)

The three children have learned to collaborate around the text and around the computer. Carl, on the other hand, sees the collaboration diminishing if there is no face-to-face interaction. But, as we saw in the previous chapter, people have indeed learned to collaborate remotely using CmC. There is an important difference that these two scenarios highlight. For the three children, the text was jointly owned. For Carl and his typist, the text is owned by Carl. The typist, even when she collaborated face-to-face, was an assistant who perhaps was recognized in the acknowledgements of Carl's final manuscript; she was not a partner, a co-author. She had more invested in making the transaction smooth and brief so she could get on with her other work. Indeed, she may have been waiting for an opportunity to spend less time on Carl's work. When writers are truly equal partners, this tension lessens and whether the collaboration is face-to-face or through CmC is less important.

Although multiple authorship and collaborative writing are not new, the notion of authorship not being a solitary undertaking only becomes a focal issue when we examine writing in the computer age. In the beginning, wordprocessing opened up the possibility for the individual author to write multiple drafts with relative ease; now, networking and the exchange of diskettes (jokingly called 'sneakernet') allows the individual to collaborate with others in the construction of the text. We can not even tell who composed which part since there is no identifying handwriting. Spell-checkers and style-checkers have removed some of the tedium of editing and, in a primitive sense, collaborate in the writing. Further, they neutralize writing through their homogenizing effects. With the advent of computer networks (as we saw in Chapter 5), teachers and students, students and students, and workers and workers collaborate to produce texts.

In my research at IBM, I found that researchers and managers collaborate online and orally to produce their texts. Online manuals and even computer programs (which usually exist in soft copy only) are constantly updated as colleagues make additions, annotations, and deletions. Multiple users append to bulletin boards and, while each contribution shows the name and location of the writer, the colleague responsible for the bulletin board can delete contributions as he sees fit. These texts vary from short notes to lengthy research reports and documents. Who then is the author of such texts? All of the contributors, the initiating author, or perhaps even the writer of the spell checker? While one person may be responsible for the maintenance of the text and the organization of changes, such texts do not appear to have the single authority of traditional print. Does this mean, then, that they exhibit the characteristics of oral language? Traditional discussion on orality and literacy claims that orality does not have authority because it is not fixed and permanent; it cannot be analysed, compared with other texts, and enter into the canons of our culture. It is too individualistic and spontaneous. The texts in this computer-mediated community in fact range from the highly spontaneous, individualistic to the highly crafted. But all appear in print, either on the screen or in a later hard copy. Can we then still hold that it is the fact that text is written that endows it with the characteristics of literacy?

While print has an analogous form in edited journals and books of papers, the question of authorship has been established over time: royalties and other payments are made according to a contractual agreement; authority is vested in the individual author as primary authority, with the editor providing 'the good housekeeping seal of approval'. The more prestigious the editor(s), the more valuable the approval; but the contribution must still stand on its own merits. No such legal or consensual status currently exists for texts produced and disseminated online. This partly explains the reluctance of some scholars and scientists to contribute to computer conferences or the increasing number of electronic journals that I discussed in the previous chapter. They have no legal copyright protection and so are cautious of sharing their work until it is published (in print).

Other researchers, mostly in educational settings, have also noted the collaborative effect of writing with a computer; students construct meaning jointly, producing a negotiated text (see, for example, Heap 1989; Kleifgen, 1991). In her early book, *Writing and Computers*, Colette Daiute (1985), one of the earliest researchers on writing with computers relates the following scenario. This scenario is already being duplicated across nations, age groups, and occupations as more and more people have come to discover the collaborative possibilities of electronic text.

Cathy was writing the personal statement for her college application. Pretending that she was talking to a long-lost aunt, she wrote quickly about what was important in her life. She did not worry about mistakes, because she knew she would be able to correct them fairly easily with the word-processing commands. Several classmates at a table near her computer were attracted by the speed and noise of her typing, so they came over to read the statement. One boy said, 'They like to hear about lots of activities. Tell them more about all the stuff you've been doing in student government and the antinuclear movement.' Another girl thought the tone was too informal: 'Organize it around themes and use anecdotes from your life to hit home some points. But don't chat.' Cathy's classmates also enjoyed catching her spelling mistakes.

(Daiute 1985, p. 19)

In fact, the collaborative effects of several students working together has lead researchers such as Daiute to recommend students be grouped around computers rather than have one computer for each student. The latter arrangement, they claim, returns us to the solitary, isolated writer model of writing and misses the collaborative opportunities the computer provides. Others, as we saw in the previous chapter, have shown that networking and electronic mail can provide this same collaboration and community of writers.

This collaboration raises important issues, however. Who is the author of such texts? (It also raises the question of the nature of the text, which I shall discuss in the next section.) If we can collaborate and also access each other's texts with ease, merging their text into ours with the touch of a few keys or the pull of a mouse, what is plagiarism? The notion of plagiarism is a current Western phenomenon, based on a belief of individual possession now enshrined in the legal concept of 'intellectual property'. The photocopy machine began to break down our social disapproval of plagiarism. The computer takes that break down further. Computer programmers and software vendors have tried without success to protect the product of their intellect by 'copy protection' techniques. Pirated software sits in most people's homes and offices. When I have been offered a 'free' program and have declined the offer, I have seen raised eyebrows from friends and colleagues who would never 'steal' an apple from a neighbour's tree.

Another feature of electronic text is that the writer can now produce 'perfect' laser printed text. The whole production process of books, through editors, copy-editors, and typesetters can be avoided. But, will the quality of such books be the same? Without the critical editor to prune my verbosity, examine my logic, and even check my sources, will my book be worth the reading? If it is, who should benefit from the savings in production cost? Book publisher or writer? Am I now author and publisher? On the other hand, we might see writing (including literature) develop online through several drafts. Just as computer programmers receive feedback on bulletin boards and alter their programs, so, too might scholars put a draft on a bulletin board, wait for the responses and incorporate them where relevant. I have no answers to these questions – these are issues that must be brought to public consciousness, discussed and debated. Although the notion of individual control over the entire writing process cheers the heart of Western individualistic societies, it raises complex issues of ownership, standards, and ultimately, money!

Popular press articles extol the advantages of desktop publishing; but I believe we need to consider the cost of this almost instant production of texts. Frederic Davis (1987), for example, says that desktop publishing will prevent scientists from duplicating each others work because, with traditional journal publication, the time lag between discovery and publication means colleagues are not aware of others conducting the same research. Further, not all research or creative writing can be published since publishers have limited budgets and so limit their output. Desktop publishing, such writers claim, will allow scientists and other academics to publish, not perish; writers will not starve in their garrets. But, the important issue for language in our social life is whether we all *want* to become publishing houses and whether it is cost effective to do so. For publishing houses, the answer is yes. One of the most prolific coffee-table products, 'Day in the Life' photo books, are desktop published, saving almost 18 months in production and printing time. To achieve such desktop publishing, Collins employs fewer people and they all must have diverse skills since they do the work of many people.

The cost for smaller, individual concerns may be too great. While it may be cheaper to desktop publish my own research, I am spending even more time on the actual production than on the research. While I gain independence from copy-editors and the like, I take on more responsibility for technical details. Will such additional labour really help the academic and the professional writer survive? While I would be prepared to publish my research less formally through an electronic conference or bulletin board, knowing that the formatting, and so on would not have to be perfect, I would prefer to have someone else copy-edit and proofread any text I produce in hard copy. For most of use, the decisions will either be taken out of our hands or will be reached according to individual interests. This option was given to me by another publishing house for my previous book. They requested (but did not demand) a camera-ready copy of the book. Since I would have to spend time converting my wordprocessing controls for another printer and would have to copyedit, proofread, create an index and so on, I declined. Although we have desktop publishing programs in our computer classrooms, and use them for student-produced newsletters, and so on, I do not see myself as a publisher; nor do I want to. I value the comments from editors and copy-editors. I know that they will respond as a real audience to my writing. Without this interaction, my writing would more likely be 'writer-based prose' than 'reader-based prose' (Flower 1979). It is important to me, and other scholars, to produce finished text that is well-crafted. When the editor of the TESOL Quarterly, Steve Gaies, resigned from the position, he received accolades from many scholars and colleagues in the profession. One well-known TESL professional recounted how Steve had worked with him over many long letters and telephone calls to produce a well-crafted article. The author then went on to say how people often came up to him and, referring to this article in the TESOL Quarterly, praised the content of the article and then commented 'You write so well. It's a pleasure to read your work.'

Probably the greatest advantage of electronic text for the individual is that I can submit my raw text document to a journal or publisher on disk. The publisher has only to format the text, thus saving input costs for the publisher and saving me from proofreading poorly typeset text. Although I submit many articles on disk (and have submitted a book), I have not seen the reading public benefit from the cost savings through lower priced books and journals.

What is more profound about the approach to self-publication is the change in control of information. No longer does an editor or a publishing house, or even a colleague acting as journal reviewer have ultimate control over *what* we say. Given the spread of CmC discussed in the previous chapter, control over *to whom* we say it can also lie in the hands of the writer, who can 'publish' electronically, as in bulletin boards.

THE NATURE OF ELECTRONIC TEXT

What do such texts themselves look like? This variable process produces malleable electronic texts, which unlike printed texts, are not fixed either in content or format. Rather, like oral texts, they are evanescent, as Ong claims. We've all seen the organization of the text change before us as we press this key to move text, or that key to delete text. While many of us use wordprocessors of the what-you-see-is-what-you-get variety, the IBM researchers and managers I studied primarily used a text formatter. Are these two texts the same? When I first wrote the paper on which this chapter is based, the last word of the previous sentence appeared at the beginning of a line, but now, in my wordprocessed version it appears almost in the middle of a line. Does this alter the text? Are they still essentially the same? Most users of wordprocessors use bold, italic, or other fonts that can not be reproduced on screen, even if they format the text to the screen so that it appears in the same ordering as in print. When they choose underline, for example, on the mainframe computers, the underline appears on a separate line of its own beneath the text to be underlined. On a PC, the text appears as a different colour. In print, the text is underscored. In the wordprocessor I am currently using, underline appears as a black box around the text. Are these essentially the same text? This may appear a trivial example; however, it illustrates the evanescent nature of online texts. Once printed, the text becomes fixed and no longer malleable. This is a new dimension to text, one that alters our traditional views of orality and literacy. The traditional view is that written text is permanent, that meaning and authority are lodged in writing, making it the suitable vehicle for rational, critical thinking. Online texts are written, but do not have the permanence of print. I have argued elsewhere (Murray 1988 and in the previous chapter) that it is not whether a particular stretch of language is written or oral that determines its nature; it is the context, that is, the interaction between the field, the setting, and the relation between speaker and hearer that determines the nature of the text and even the choice of medium (face-to-face, pen and ink, telephone, print, or computer).

Electronic texts are not only infinitely variable, but are also artificially (though not permanently) bounded. We still use the metaphors of previous print technology when we talk about 'paging down', but these 'pages' are artificial in the digitized world;

they map a possible print version. We are caught in a double bind when we treat the electronic page as a printed page. First, the printed page on most monitors does not map the screen page; it is very frustrating not being able to see the entire page (in the printed sense) on the same screen. Evidently, it is not sufficiently frustrating for people to pay for the monitors that do display a page on the screen as you type. While these monitors do exist, they are very expensive and, thus far, have not sold well. Even though we continue to use print metaphors when talking about the text on screen, because the text is ever-changing, we can no longer use the memory cues we have internalized for retrieving information from printed text. We cannot say 'Oh, I remember reading about that. It was on the top right-hand page of this document.' In equating electronic text to printed text, we are confined by modes of thinking from a different technology. Thus far, even computer professionals have not developed new ways of accessing information that we encoded visually and spatially in print. Of course, we have the marvellous 'search' facility in electronic text; but we must be able to recall an exact word or phrase, not just a concept. But, what of the possibilities the computer provides? We could have hypermedia with graphics and even sound, that is, online text from which we can access other texts, graphics, sound and compact disks. The very nature of text is likely to change if we forget any analogy with print. Reading *David Copperfield* online could mean calling up scenes from the movie, or calling up music of the Victorian era, or viewing a short movie of life in the Fen country, or listening to the sounds of the storm on the Suffolk coast. This is intertextuality at the touch of a keystroke.

Computer text is public as well as being personal and immediate because it can be my unorganized spontaneous thoughts and yet appear in type. Just as the typewritten letter was once not considered the proper vehicle for personal letters, so too many people object to electronically produced letters. (I have one friend who always hand-writes her letters, and another who apologizes for using a wordprocessor.) The art and culture of letter writing gave way to mechanized writing, which is now giving way to the merged form letter. We can no longer know whether our friends' letter to us is the same as the one to other friends. It can appear personal, with a merged header and salutation. But, how many other merges went on? Am I truly the 'you' of the letter?

A variety of genres appear as texts in the computer. They are not all rational, analytical, integrated, or context-free. In bulletin boards, the texts resemble letters, often arguing for or against a particular issue. They resemble oral language more than written text, or the broadsides and pamphlets of earlier centuries. I can imagine a twentieth-century Martin Luther appending his Articles to a bulletin board. Other texts are fragmented notes, again more like oral language than written. Others are well-crafted, exhibiting the characteristics traditionally associated with literacy. They exhibit complex grammatical forms, voice and diction. Yet, all appear in a printed format on the screen. Although we have had oral-like written genres before (such as family letters), scholars have not paid attention to them in their discussion of orality and literacy, rather preferring to use as their examples, the prototypical cases of academic prose and oral casual conversation, two very different cases that lead us to believe the differences were the result of the medium – written or oral. Interestingly, casual, oral-like genres have become accepted into the canon as literature, for example, Pepys' Diary, Samuel Johnson's letters, and Lincoln's speeches. Despite this acceptance of oral genres, research and discussion on orality and literacy, as I discussed in Chapter 2, have focused on academic prose and casual conversation. With the texts available online, we can no longer ignore the variety of genres available in both media. Were Homer's texts of any less literary merit when they were oral sung poetry before becoming written and frozen?

Since, as we have seen, many texts never see hard copy, appearing in soft copy only without the attention to detail given to printed texts (there are few editors and copy-editors of electronic texts) many electronic texts have non-standard syntax, punctuation, and, despite spell-checkers, spelling. During my research at IBM I observed hundreds (if not thousands) of electronic texts. While some people carefully crafted their texts since they never knew who would read them, others equated electronic text with speech, producing text on the fly, with typographic errors, infelicities and so on that have their equivalences in the hesitations, malapropisms, and other speech errors of the spoken language. Most of these texts, however, were not public language. I once received an inspection copy of a software program for teaching grammar and vocabulary to second language speakers that had both syntax and spelling errors in the screen displays students would read. Needless to say, I did not purchase the software. The Consumer Service screen displays I referred to in the first chapter are public and exhibit idiosyncratic punctuation/spelling. Two of the screens are represented below. In addition to idiosyncratic punctuation and syntax, they also demonstrate a mixture of register, from the casual 'Hi' to the formal 'if you desire' to jargon 'item availability'.

SCREEN 2

WELCOME TO THE SILENT SERVICE ORDERING SYSTEM,

PLEASE ENTER AREA CODE AND PHONE NUMBER
(MUST BE 10 DIGITS NO SPACES PLEASE)

OR PRESS THE GREEN KEY TO BEGIN AGAIN. THANK YOU!

SCREEN 4

HI! I'M SILENT SERVICE

YOUR PERSONAL ORDERING SYSTEM

IF YOU WOULD LIKE TO CHECK ITEM AVAILABILITY OR ORDER AN
ITEM TYPE IN THE CATALOG NUMBER AND PRESS THE BLUE KEY

IF YOU DESIRE TO BEGIN AGAIN PLEASE PRESS THE GREEN KEY

Electronic text makes ready to hand the intertextuality of text. All texts are connected to other texts in a web of meaning, genre, style, players and situation. In printed texts, this intertextuality is hidden, connected in the mind of the reader, or explicated through footnotes and bibliographies. To access connected texts, the reader has to search his own or others' memory, or delve into libraries, pore through other printed texts in search of a hidden relation. But, it is this interconnectedness of texts that creates the cultural background against which society functions. With hypertext, developed by Ted Nelson, cross-references and links can be accessed at the touch of a button. As I read a text online, I can access any one of a number of connections the reader coded. For example, if this were an electronic hypertext, you could now, with the touch of some symbol attached to Ted Nelson's name, read about how he developed hypertext, read his own books in which he makes a wonderful attempt to represent hypertext in print. Or, you could access hypercard, Apple Computer's variety of hypertext, moving from hypertext to the Macintosh, to window interfaces, to Allan Kay formerly of Xerox and now of Apple, who developed the window interface and so on *ad infinitum*. You could, as reader, encode your own associations, connections, references and comments into hypertext. In a very real way, the 'reader' can become part of the socio-cultural world in which the text is embedded. 'If the program allows the reader to make changes in the text or to add his own connections (as some hypertext systems do), then the game becomes still more complex. The reader becomes his own author' (Bolter 1989, p. 142), a situation similar to that in many oral traditions, where the audience interaction leads the storyteller to add or remove sections from the story.

ELECTRONIC TEXT AND AUDIENCE

And I hate for anyone to see something full of typos . . . You can type so fast now, you fly with these new machines. But what it looks like before you correct it! And what a table looks like before you format it! My boss would get scared if he saw it on the screen. He'd think his secretary had started writing in hieroglyphics . . . So what I do, if I'm halfway through something, let's say I did a rough draft but didn't have a chance to edit or run the spell check – I used to be such a perfect speller before I got this thing – if I'd be embarrassed to have somebody see it half done, I change the document's title to something like XMASMEMO. Especially if it's for Mr. _____. If he's going through my files, he'll never find it . . . When it's ready, I change it back to BdSchd8/2 [board schedule] . . . If they can't find it then they have to come to me and ask. That way I can neaten it up before I print it out. The other way I would always be making my unfinished work look finished, which would really be a waste of time. It's more efficient to format afterwards on a lot of these things.

(Garson 1988, pp. 213–14)

Ceal Paoli, whom Garson is reporting here, clearly shows how important audience is for her when she is writing. With her audience clearly in mind, she makes accommodations without changing her own preferred writing style of leaving editing until last.

This brings me to the fourth focus of text – audience. Literary and rhetorical studies have always recognized the importance of audience in the writing process. Given the importance of audience to any writer, it is surprising that less research and theory exists around the question of how the relationship between author and audience changes with the computer. Computer technology provides the opportunity for interactive text, a combination that earlier scholars would no doubt have considered an oxymoron. For example, Professor Rob Swigart at San José State University has developed interactive fiction using the Macintosh. The reader (participant?) in the story can makes choices at various stages in the narrative, thus constructing a different version of the story each time it is read. Author and audience interact via the text.

Within business communities, writer and audience interact through text. The writer is very conscious of the intended audience and also considers the unintentional audience, the person who may be carbon copied. In many cases people forward received memos, and so on to others. In some instances, after being forwarded many times over, it will return to the originator! Several people I studied received e-mail or a document they had originated and to which someone had added, 'Have you seen this?' The IBM community is very sensitive to this issue and many writers carefully construct even the most casual note. However, people differ in their responses to the possibility of an unintentional audience. Others told me they choose e-mail because of its lack of conventions that allow them to be more spontaneous and so get away with things they would not be able to in telephone calls, paper memos, and so forth, as we saw in detail in the last chapter. Although, for example, e-mail is a major medium of communication because of the problems of telephone tag, many people do not address e-mail to colleagues they know do not like or use the medium. Although less and less appears in hard copy, it is used either as back-up, or for legal reasons. Contracts, for example, are negotiated online, but the final copy for signature is printed. Signatures are the only authentication currently accepted by our legal system, which is the audience for such contracts. That, too, will change when we have devised a reliable online authentication system.

As the audience, intended or otherwise, responds, the writer changes the text, or responds with another text, clarifying, exemplifying, explaining. As in face-to-face conversations, a dialogue develops around the text and out of the text. Often the original text is no longer the focus since the focus shifts to accommodate the demands of the audience.

The reader of online texts is no longer solitary and isolated as with printed texts. In traditional Western print culture, reading is valued as an individual, often silent, activity. Just as writing is considered a private, intimate act, so too is reading. Even in the most totalitarian state, reader and writer can create their own worlds through the text. Within this cultural perspective, the book symbolizes individualism. However, even within Western nations, literacy events are not necessarily solitary. Shirley Brice Heath, in *Ways with Words* (1984), describes two communities in the United States for whom literacy is a shared, collaborative enterprise. Electronic text, as we have seen encourages such cooperation and collaboration.

WHAT DOES THE COMPUTER AS TEXT PROCESSOR TELL US?

This examination of the computer as text processor has raised a number of theoretical and practical issues concerning text in an electronic era. While the computer has liberated us from the tedium of revising and editing, it lures us into seeing private text as public, into writing to the printer and not the audience, into paying attention to surface detail while forgetting the overall coherence of our text, into playing with fonts rather than ideas. For those of us grounded in a print tradition, the move to electronic text can be liberating or terrifying. We can be free to produce our own desktop published books or we can be rendered powerless to act, resisting the very idea of changing our view of self and text, as Michelle (p. 99) does. Steeped in our own traditions of learning, literacy, and language, we can overlook the creative uses of a number of media that our children like Tanya (p. 112) and employees like Ceal (p. 123) bring with them. Even more importantly, if writing is a way for minds to touch, we must be ever sensitive to the needs of our audience, ever conscious that we write to find meaning.

Just as our notions of literacy are challenged by the different literacies described by scholars such as Heath, Scribner and Cole, and Street (see Chapter 2), so too, the use of electronic media to produce, store and transmit texts challenges us to rethink our traditional view of the dichotomy between orality and literacy. Rather, we need an integrated approach for examining oral and written language, an approach grounded in the view that literacy and orality are social practices whose forms and functions vary for different social groups, and that electronic text is but another category in our language repertoire.

FOR DISCUSSION

1. This chapter has raised the issue of ownership and therefore of plagiarism. In what ways should 'intellectual property' produced electronically be protected?
2. This chapter has shown the limitations of style checkers. What kinds of knowledge about language do style checkers need to 'know' in order to be more useful to writers?
3. In what ways can beautiful text production 'seduce' the writer into believing the text is well written?
4. How does hypertext map or not the way you read by association?

FOR ACTION

1. Interview a friend or colleague who is both a good writer and computer user. Ask him/her about his/her writing process. Where/how do they plan, pre-write, write, revise? How has their writing process changed with the use of the wordprocessor?
2. Try to use a new wordprocessor, one that you have never tried before. How different is it from using your usual one? How do these differences impede or enhance your writing process?
3. Interview an editor in a publishing house or of a magazine or journal. Ask them about how much electronic means they use in their production. Do contributors submit copy online, on disk,

on paper? How do they typeset? Do they use spell checkers, style checkers, idea processors?

4. Select a well-known fairy tale. Write it as if for a hypertext program. Insert different branches and selections during the story.

FURTHER READING

Daiute (1985) provides an excellent study of wordprocessing among children. Heim (1987) has the most thorough philosophical discussion of wordprocessing. Hawisher and Selfe (1991) and Gerrard (1987) are both thought-provoking collections of articles of the future possibilities for writing and writing instruction using computers. The journal, *Text and Technology*, formerly, *The Wordprocessing Newsletter*, is a good source of recent issues and periodically publishes a bibliography on wordprocessing. The journal *Computers and Composition* is a journal for teachers of writing.

SEVEN

The computer as knowledge broker

> Knowledge is of two kinds – we know a subject ourselves or we know where we can find information upon it.
>
> *Ben Jonson*

THE INFORMATION AGE

Computer-based technology is often called information technology, giving rise to the name, 'the information age'. Why the focus on information? In a 1990 interview about the twenty-first century with Edward Reingold, management consultant Peter Drucker stated that

> Most people are no longer part of the business society; they are part of the knowledge society. If you go back to when your father was born and mine, knowledge was an ornament, a luxury – and now it is the very center.

(Reingold 1990, p. 6)

Whether it is in our work, our recreation, or any other part of our lives, we are overwhelmed with more and more information – the growth has been exponential. With this growth has come a critical need to store information so that it is readily accessible. The individual even in Jonson's day was not able to 'know' everything. What is important is to know where to find it, be able to find it, and be able to use it. Earlier this century, before the use of computers in the public arena, we would know the place and person who had the information.

Along with this growth in the amount of information and our need for it, has come a change in who holds the information and the question of how we can access it. Knowledge was once the province of the scholar-priest. With the advent of the printing press, the printing shop and the bookstore became the sources of knowledge. The nineteenth century saw the introduction, in the Western world, of the public library. Access to information became a virtually universal social service in Western countries. Now, computer professionals and commercial enterprises control the databases that hold the information. Services like Prodigy, CompuServe, America Online as well as government and academic research organizations contain and provide access to vast amounts of information, but at a price well beyond the means of most individuals. The (electronic) 'public library' does not exist in the information age.

> The city as we know it is obsolete. It is a 19th century product based on our 19th century ability to move people. Moving ideas and information then was more difficult, and the great inventions of the 19th century were the streetcar and the post office. Today we have an incredible ability to move ideas and information, but the movement of people is grinding to a standstill.
>
> (Drucker in Reingold 1990)

This chapter considers computer technology in the same way Jonson described our human use of knowledge – computers as repositories of information that we access; and computers as 'intelligent', capable of knowing and using the information. This chapter, then, will be organized around these two facets of computer-based technology.

INFORMATION SOURCE

As we go about our daily lives, we continually encounter computers that provide us with the information we need. To access this information, we first have to deal with the computer interface and then with the way the information has been organized by the programmer.

At the computer interface

Compare the two approaches to the computer interface in the following scenarios.

Example 1

Sears Department Store has a mail order service. Using Prodigy, an online information service, I can make my order by typing in my request onto an online form. I must supply information about the item from the company catalog and information about where to ship it, and my credit card number for payment. I can then choose to have it delivered to my house (with an additional delivery charge), or go to the nearest store and pick it up in person. If I decide to pick it up in person, I go to the Catalog ordering department and am confronted with a computer with a touch screen, which says:

Screen 1:

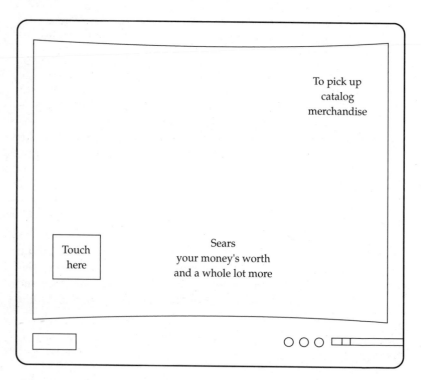

Screen 2:

	Please enter your	
	7-digit telephone number	
1	2	3
4	5	6
7	8	9
*	0	clear

Telephone number gets written in below the instructions as you type. You get a feedback beep with each number you touch.

Screen 3:

Is this your telephone number?
555-4323

| Yes | | No |

Screen 4:

To locate your catalog
merchandise please go to
catalog assistance counter

I received this message because I had not ordered anything. If I had, I would have been given the aisle and shelf number where I could then collect my merchandise, take it to the cashier, pay for it, and leave the store.

The following example is the one I discussed in Chapter 1. A local discount store, Consumer Service, has a computerized order system to make the transaction faster. I can make my order via the terminal, or by going to a clerk at the checkout. In either case, I then have to go to the customer pick-up counter to collect the merchandise. If I ordered through Silent Service, I need to pay at the pick-up counter. If I ordered through the clerk, he has already taken my payment.

Example 2
Screen 1

```
                    SILENT SERVICE
                1) SILENT SERVICE ORDERING
                2) MAILING LIST UPDATE
    PLEASE ENTER YOUR CHOICE (1 OR 2) THEN PRESS THE BLUE KEY
```

Screen 2

```
            WELCOME TO THE SILENT SERVICE ORDERING SYSTEM,
    PLEASE ENTER AREA CODE AND PHONE (MUST BE 10 DIGITS NO SPACES PLEASE)
        OR PRESS THE GREEN KEY TO BEGIN AGAIN. THANK-YOU!
```

Screen 3

AREA CODE AND PHONE (408) 555-4323
ENTER Y IF YOU AGREE, OR N IF NO.

Screen 4

HI! I'M SILENT SERVICE
YOUR PERSONAL ORDERING SYSTEM
IF YOU WOULD LIKE TO CHECK ITEM AVAILABILITY OR ORDER AN ITEM
TYPE IN THE CATALOG NUMBER AND PRESS THE BLUE KEY

IF YOU DESIRE TO BEGIN AGAIN PLEASE PRESS THE GREEN KEY

Screen 5

CATALOG NUMBER: ITEM DESCRIPTION:
CURRENT SELL PRICE:

YES - YOUR ITEM IS AVAILABLE

TO ORDER ENTER A QUANTITY 1-9, OTHERWISE PRESS THE BLUE KEY TO CONTINUE

ENTER 'Y' IF YOU HAVE ADDITIONAL ITEMS TO ORDER
'N' IF NOT

Screen 6

YOUR ORDER IS FOR

QUANTITY   ITEM NUMBER   DESCRIPTION   PRICE

ENTER Y IF YOU AGREE, N IF NOT

Notes: 'Yes' and 'No' are at the usual 'Y' and 'N' keys but are coloured red and also have 'Yes' and 'No' on them. The blue key has 'ENTER' on it. The green key has 'SEND' on it. Infelicities of syntax, etc. are as in the system.

Clearly, interfaces such as these, used for single domain operations and by people with perhaps minimal computer familiarity, should be as transparent as their alternative – a catalog and a telephone. Consumer Services' interface is visually difficult to navigate, requires keyboard use, and gives unclear directions. The Sears interface, on the other hand, is visually simple, requires only pointing at the screen, and gives clear directions, without talking down to the customer. In both cases, however, the non-literate consumer is unable to use this facility. For now, both companies give such a consumer an alternative – a store clerk. But, as more and more companies computerize operations to reduce their costs, we will see more computers and fewer people. This transformation has already occurred in the banking industry where automatic tellers (with no clerical back-up) are now the major method used by customers for conducting banking transactions. Although some ATMs are aware that language is involved (my on-campus ATM, for example, giving the customer the choice between English and Spanish), none seem to have recognized that literacy is a requirement *and* that customers may be confused by the banking terminology used, such as 'primary savings', 'transaction', 'fast withdrawal'. Nor is there even consistency within the industry – some use 'personal identification number', others use 'password'. All are codes impenetrable to many users. This impenetrability is exacerbated in more complex services such as the online services. Current discussion about the advantages of the information super highway only talk about the number of possible television channels – 500; or the speed of information retrieval – 14,400 bits per second. They do not discuss the fact that its current prototype, the Internet, does not have an indexing system or cataloging system even remotely close in power and sophistication to what our libraries have in the Dewey Decimal or Library of Congress systems. Nor do they discuss that a recent survey in the United States (Boyd 1994) found that 23 per cent of Americans are 'not comfortable' using a computer. These numbers increase for older people, women and minorities.

When we are looking at usability research, we have to remember that we are not simply looking at a small part of a huge system in isolation. The operation is holistic; the reading of a text on a screen (or anywhere) depends entirely on the place of the text and the reader in a system which may have links which are not obvious.

(Hunt and Vassiliadis 1988, p. 140)

Retrieval of information

I subscribe to an online information service. Imagine the following. I want to find out the time of flights between San José and Los Angeles. I first log into the service, using a userid and password. I then get the menu of available services. I select 'travel'. Then another menu of various travel options comes up. I select 'airlines'. Then comes another menu. I select reservations. I get a fill-in form online and put in the date of travel from San José. I then get a screen full of times of flights. I back out of that screen and again call up the reservations menu. I type in the date of my return and get a screen full of times of flights. I back out again and then choose airfares from the reservations menu. I check the airfares and then go to the screens that explain the various codes attached to each fare – whether it has a Saturday night stay over, etc. At this point, I suddenly realize that maybe, if I left earlier in the day, I could get a cheaper flight. But, how do I get back to the information that was on my screen only moments ago? Do I have to keep backing out until I get the reservations menu again?

The previous section only dealt with very simple information and the design of the computer interface. If the information we want to retrieve is more complex, the question of retrieval becomes crucial.

Researchers who have examined people's interaction with the computer interface have agreed that a system must have consistent external behaviour – behaviour independent of its internal workings. The user is not interested in, nor needs to know, *how* the system operates. In order to achieve this invisibility of the system's workings, Apple Computer introduced the Macintosh interface, using the pull-down menu system and the office and desktop as a metaphor. The pull-down menu system remains constant for all applications, providing the interface with consistent external behaviour. And, we can place documents in folders that can be placed in file drawers. Even the earlier DOS-based personal computer systems used 'files' as a metaphor for individual documents stored in the computer. Like all metaphors, the office works both for and against the person trying to use the interface. When we want to access information, whether in a folder or a file, we still need to recall how we named our document and in which folder we placed it. The more documents we have, the more difficult it is to remember and therefore retrieve what we need. In addition, filing systems are idiosyncratic, as anyone who has tried to find a document in someone else's filing cabinet or computer can attest. Many people are able to 'file' information and documents in apparent random distribution over their desktop; others create elaborate naming systems with subcategories. People who use the former method are most disadvantaged in trying to use a computer filing system because much of their retrieval is visually based and spatially orientated. Even those who create elaborate filing systems rely on visual cues. We remember that the file (or document) we are looking for is somewhere in the back of this hanging file and it was an article from a popular magazine. With this information, we have spatial and visual cues about what we are looking for. But, on the computer, information becomes standardized. All files look alike and there is no such thing as 'the back of a hanging file'. In some systems, we can order our files by date. This can be a great help. Just as the person who files things all over their desk can retrieve information quickly, based on both the place where they put it and the time, we can also often recall *when* we used or wrote the computer file, even if we can not recall what we called it.

Thus, if computers are to work to help us store information, they must also work to help us to access that information. One recent innovation that is designed to support access to information is hypertext. Traditionally, information, which is available as text, has been presented on the printed page that we generally read in a linear order. When similar information was entered into computers, it was displayed as online text, still in a linear format. When I buy a new program for my computer and install it at home, the manual often comes both online and in hard copy. But, the online manual is essentially the same as the hard copy one. Instead of scanning through paper pages and indexes, I scan through electronic pages and indexes. Most research has found that people access such information more effectively in print than on the screen. We are used to the page size of our printed document, we have the ability to remember approximately where (spatially) in the book certain material lies and we can rapidly scan and flip around the text with ease holding our place with a finger or scraps of paper. We are certainly less familiar with the representation of text on the screen. But now, rather than taking the linear blocks of textual information, online texts are presented in hypertexts that link individual sections of the text and link texts to other texts.

In hypertext, if I am reading an article about artificial intelligence and come across a reference to another book or article, I can immediately access that original book or article. If the text is computer documentation, I can choose different paths through it, depending on whether I am a novice computer user or an expert. If I am new to computers, I can check definitions, examples and advice. If I am more familiar with them, I can bypass all the sections I already know. The choice can be ours or the system itself can define different paths for different levels of expertise. But, such information structures assume that we know what information we need and in what order or that the computer programmer can predict what paths and associations we will want to make. Often, we are very vague about what information we need and even less certain about how to go about getting it. When we read a book, we assume that the author has an organizational plan, which we usually follow. However, if we know the subject well, we often do not follow the author's order at all. Although I choose a textbook for use in my graduate classes, I rarely follow the chapter sequence, but rather choose the ones I feel are most appropriate and in the order I want to present the information. In this book, for example, I have chosen a specific ordering of the chapters, with a particular model of information building on previous information in mind. However, I am sure many readers will first read the chapter that interests them most. Some hypertext systems allow users to establish their own links as they proceed through the material and thus be able to retrace their steps and associations on subsequent readings.

These issues all revolve around the most fundamental assumption on which hypertext is designed – that hypertexts are more natural, more like human thinking than linear texts. This assumption is based on the view that human memory is associative and that we can process information more easily if it is presented in a network. However, much knowledge is organized and processed hierarchically and linearly by the human mind. Indeed, some researchers (e.g., Just and Carpenter 1987) claim that it is the human brain, not the linear printed text that constrains our facility for accessing information. As mentioned in Chapter 2, reading research shows that we build schemata as we read; we recreate our mental representations (schema) as we acquire new information. This research also shows that, if the text is ill-formed (e.g., disorganized), it is more difficult to recreate our schemata. Readers rely on text organization to help them access the information. They expect and use organizers such as headings and overviews; they expect and use cohesive devices. They expect a text that is coherent within their cultural framework. Western writing expects the writer to provide these cues for the reader. But, in hypertext, we expect the reader to do this. Moreover, experts in the knowledge domain of the text can create representations when the text is organized in an unpredictable manner. Novices in the knowledge domain can not. Therefore, it is even more important for the information to be organized in an expected manner for any information retrieval since it is most often novices who are seeking the new information.

Contrastive rhetoric has shown that a linear form of rhetorical organization is Western, and largely American (Kaplan, 1966; Kaplan et al. 1983). Therefore, I would argue that hypertext is doing nothing different from, say, what Kaplan calls Japanese rhetoric, which expects the reader to make assumptions and draw his or her own conclusions. However, even though Japanese texts expect more of the reader, the writer still must produce a coherent text – it is merely that the rules for how to achieve this are different.

As readers try to navigate though the hypertext (or, for that matter, imbedded menu systems), they lose track of where they are and how to go back or forward. We saw this in the voice-mail systems, Given that menu and hypertext systems are far more complex than any voice-mail systems, there exist far more opportunities for getting lost, as in the very simple example of the airline reservation system scenario at the beginning of this section. In an era of information overload, when our jobs and often our lives depend on our ability to find and use information, we need to be able to access easily the information when we need it.

There are a variety of on-line services that can provide us with information – but which has what information? Once I try to use such a database, how simple is it for me to get the actual information I want? How many layers of menus do I have to work through or how many hypertext branches do I have to follow? Internet alone has many thousands of formal information sources – how can I tell which one will be of interest to me? Several information 'agents' have been developed, such as Gopher, which literally 'goes for' whatever the user asks for. 'With Gopher, you can tunnel through the Internet and boldly go where no user has suspected he could go before' (Gibbs and Smith, 1993, p. 135). If I want information on a particular topic, for example, 'security', my Gopher directs all Gophers it knows about to send back lists of items related to security. In this example, the list is relatively small. If, however, I ask for information on a more general topic (e.g., language), I could get back so much information that the entire system would be clogged with answers to my request. Gophers also provide menus listing topics of information. I can then ask the Gopher to go to one site that has information I am interested in. I check the information, which might direct me to yet another source, which in turn can direct me to yet another source, and so on. This works like an endless catalogue or index system, with each index card pointing to yet another card. In one such case, I ended up back at the very computer I was initially logged onto. Although tools such as Gopher make it easier to get information because the tool itself types in all the different computer addresses where the information might be, it has major restrictions. The success of the search depends on how many other Gopher systems mine knows about, how specific I am in defining the information I want, and whether the people running the systems have catalogued the information using the same name I have. We have all experienced this same frustration with indexes at the back of books. With the Internet, this frustration is multiplied because the amount of information is so great.

Once I find it, how can I use that information? How can I make it part of a recreation of my mental representations? These are vital issues that have still not been addressed adequately by the makers of databases or online services. The ideal, of course, would be for the system to evaluate our individual preferences and then provide menus and data that accommodate our preferences. But, given, as we shall see later, that eliciting this knowledge from one human being by another is difficult and error prone, we are not likely to find such customized databases in the near future. The best we might hope for is that connections are made transparent to the user and that the user always knows where exactly she is in relation to all other possibilities of where she might have come from and be going to. Otherwise, it is rather like trying to drive the Los Angeles freeways with no map *and* no street signs.

INTELLIGENT MACHINE?

We do not need to go far to open a newspaper or magazine and find a discussion about, or advertisement for, expert systems or artificial intelligence. The debate about the potential, the desirability and even the possibility of artificial intelligence is long and often bitter. This debate has not been aided by the persistently unfulfilled claims of many of artificial intelligence's strong proponents or the fictional fears engendered by deranged HALs (the HAL 9000 computer depicted in the film *2001: A Space Odyssey*). Nevertheless, the desire remains strong for the tirelessly patient teacher, the selflessly obedient soldier, the technical expert with the instantly correct answer and the simultaneous interpreter with fluency in Japanese. But, before presenting these issues, most of which deal with language and human knowing, imagine the following scenarios.

> At Du Pont, the chemical giant, a customer calls, wanting the company to produce the ideal packaging material for their new food product. Du Pont workers ask the customer for details about how the packaging will be used and what it will contain, questions about shelf life, humidity, transparency, lid foil, thickness of the packaging wall, whether the contents are inert, liquid, solid and so. The workers enter this information into a computer; the computer processes the information and recommends the ideal packaging material and its cost.

> You are on a round-the-world two-month vacation trip. During your travels, you have been using several different credit cards, trying not to overspend your limits on each. It is now the last week of your vacation and, in a store in Santa Fé, New Mexico, you see an antique Navajo Rug, better than any you have seen before. But, it is $3,000 and you know you are probably already up to your limit on your American Express Card. And, you have not even paid the previous month's bill because you were travelling at the time. You decide to

buy the rug, and give the saleswoman your AmEx Card. She runs it through the automatic card approval machine. Unbeknown to you, at the AmEx Center in Phoenix, the computer registers that this purchase would take you over your credit limit. Immediately, an authorizer, who works all day in front of a computer screen receives several screens full of data, with the advice message 'recommend credit be extended; customer shows evidence of travelling, which may account for the outstanding balance'. The authorizer sends back to the store in Santa Fé, 'transaction authorized'. The authorizer is using an expert system that immediately analyses your credit history and makes recommendations.

Artificial intelligence

As with most metaphors, the term 'artificial intelligence' is misleading. Since cognitive psychologists and others still debate the meaning of *human* intelligence, how can we define what is meant by *artificial* intelligence? Most artificial intelligence (AI) definitions skirt the issue entirely by applying Turing's famous test as the principle for determining whether a machine's behaviour is intelligent or not. Turing's test states that if we can not tell the difference between a machine's behaviour and that of a human, the machine is intelligent. In other words, AI researchers do not try to prove that their machines or programs have intelligence, only that they behave indistinguishably from humans. This definition has led AI researchers to focus, at various times with varying emphasis and success, on two outstanding aspects of human behaviour:

1. The ability to 'recognize' complex patterns (as a euphemism for 'understand').
2. The ability to 'solve problems' (as a euphemism for 'creativity').

Can machines mimic human behaviour and behave like humans? I will argue that, in small, limited domains, they can. But, the prospect of the fully human-like HAL or R2D2 (or R2D2's linguistically impressive companion C3P0, as depicted in the film *Star Wars*) is certainly not immediate or, according to many theorists and researchers, even possible. We do not yet have a complete description of human language that will allow programming so that we can interact with machines using natural language. Our knowledge of human intelligence, while limited, shows that the way we solve problems and go about our everyday lives is not amenable to strictly logical, rule-governed processes. And, as human beings, we have world knowledge that we use to make our decisions and go about out lives. For computers to behave like humans, they must be able to use human language (usually referred to as 'natural language' to distinguish it from programming languages such as PASCAL or FORTRAN), probably human intellectual processing, and have world knowledge. How can computers know a human language?

Early work with natural language processing used the keyboard as the conduit for language; thus, programs only had to model written human language input in completely 'computer compatible' form. Another thrust of AI research has been the input (scanning) and recognition of printed and handwritten text. But, the ideal of artificial intelligence is the use of voice. We talk to the computer and it talks to us. Before examining grammar processing, speech recognition and speech synthesis (output by machine), we will examine an early AI program.

An early simulation: ELIZA

One of the earliest and most famous AI programs, ELIZA, demonstrates quite effectively how computers can be programmed to function reasonably well in small domains and yet have virtually no knowledge of natural language processing. While our understanding of language and natural language processing has come a long way since Weisenbaum developed ELIZA, I use it because it is a transparent illustration of the problems and possibilities of discourse. ELIZA is a Rogerian therapist. People with problems were invited to sit at a computer terminal and consult ELIZA, using the keyboard for input and the screen for output. Such a consultation might go like this

Patient:	I'm worried about comps [comprehensive examinations].
ELIZA:	Is it because you are worried about comps that you came to me?
Patient:	Not really.
ELIZA:	Can you expand on that?
Patient:	Well, I'm just worried about the comps?
ELIZA:	How long have you been worried about the comps?
Patient:	All semester.

ELIZA: Please don't be so short with me.
Patient: I've been worried all semester.
ELIZA: I am not sure I understand you fully.
Patient: I fell sick and tired of studying.
ELIZA: You say you fell sick and tired of studying.
Patient: Yes.
ELIZA: Why are you so positive?

Although the program appears to mimic human conversation, from the above dialogue, we can see that the responses are based on a pattern recognition process. If the patient uses a key word or phrase, ELIZA 'responds' with a predetermined sentence pattern incorporating the key word or phrase. Thus, for example, 'I am worried about comps' is embedded in the question 'Is it because XXX that you came to me?' Note that ELIZA has been programmed to change 'I' to 'you' and make appropriate verb changes, converting a statement into a question. In addition to these pattern matches and grammatical substitutions, ELIZA has also been programmed to use stock phrases if the patient's comment is difficult to match or is a brief one-word statement such as 'yes'. So, in the above dialogue, ELIZA uses stock phrases such as 'Why are you so positive?' and 'Can you elaborate on that?' Other stock responses include 'Please go on'. 'What does that suggest to you?', 'I see. Please go on'. and 'I am not sure I understand you fully'. All the responses, whether pattern matching or stock phrases give the impression that ELIZA is thinking thoughtfully. But when the patient makes an error, such as 'I fell sick' for 'I feel sick', the program, because it is merely pattern matching, picks up and uses the error. Also, the conversion of 'I am' to 'You are' can lead to absurdities such as the following:

ELIZA: You are being a bit negative.
Patient: Am i?
ELIZA: Do you believe you are?

Or, substitution can lead to the following:

ELIZA: Why do you say that?
Patient: You're crazy.
ELIZA: Perhaps you are crazy, eh?

Weizenbaum never intended his program to be used as a true artificial therapist; yet many people did believe his program worked and different versions were developed and used.

Such pattern matching programs have severe limitations. For machines to understand and produce language, they must be able to process natural language at the morpho-syntactic, semantic, and discourse levels. For spoken language, the system also needs to process language at the phonetic and phonological level.

Parsers

For machines to be able to understand (recognize) and produce language, they need a program called a parser, which takes an incoming string of natural language and analyses the structure to transform potentially ambiguous language into unambiguous representations that a computer can work with. The parser works in stages, the data being tagged by hand for lexical categorization and then the program develops parse trees based on those tags and the left-to-right structure of the clause. Although some work is being done to try to make the tagging automatic, that is, programming the machine to do the tagging, these efforts have so far been unsuccessful.

Top-down parsers try to match grammar rules against the input string, starting at the sentence level and moving lower. If the rules at a particular level fail, the parser goes back to the previous level and tries another rule. This trial and error approach slows down the parsing. Also, top-down parsers do not work very well with ill-formed input, requiring additional programming that determines which of several different parsers is best. Bottom-up parsers start by combining the lowest level constituents first and then building up to larger ones. They generate many superfluous parses and the best can only be determined after all the parses have been performed. A third approach, deterministic parsing, starts at the bottom, but, instead of trying all possibilities at that level, looks ahead to decide what is the most likely choice at the next level. All parsers use rules and there are a variety of different formalisms that represent different theories of the structure of language.

A parser is essential for any natural language processing, whether input and output are via voice, a keyboard, mouse, or any other device. Today's natural language parsers are not up to the demands of normal human speech, but progress has been made in the translation of text from the days when 'out of sight, out of mind' was rendered 'invisible and insane'. However, because they rely primarily on syntactic information, they have difficulty parsing ambiguous or ill-formed input. The sentence, 'The chickens are ready to eat', has two possible parses. Only from context do humans know whether we are on a chicken farm or ready to sit down to dinner and eat the chickens our host has prepared.

Some natural language systems run a check of nearby vocabulary to determine which of the two (or more) parses is most likely. So, if nearby sentences included words like chicken feed, the system might choose the chicken farm scenario. But, the mere presence of the word 'farm' might not produce the appropriate parse since we might be visiting cousins on a farm and they have killed some of their best chickens for our dinner. These are just some of the myriad issues in natural language processing.

Machine translation

In some strictly limited domains, most notably in highly formalized technical fields, text language translator programs can consistently achieve an accuracy of over 80 per cent. In Japan, for example, IBM-Japan translates most of its manuals using its SHALT computer. One such system, METEO translates weather reports from English to French in Canada. The system works with about a 10 per cent error margin, mainly because in such a very limited domain, the vocabulary, syntax and semantic possibilities are very limited. The translation of less structured written language (like letters, memos, essays) is far less accurate, despite newspaper headlines such as 'Towering Over Babel: *Linguist's* Software Produces Programs that Translate 260 Languages' (Gargan 1944). The *Linguist* is software that produces fonts and typographical programs for many of the world's languages. It does *not* translate.

There are three major approaches to machine translation: direct, transfer and interlingua. The direct method involves mapping from the source language directly to the target language, with no meaning processing. Consequently, they are usually limited to one target language for each source language. For the transfer approach, the source language is mapped structurally and then onto an abstract meaning representation of the target language, before being mapped onto the target language structurally. In the interlingua approach, the source language maps onto an abstract meaning representation of the source language, regardless of what the target language might be. This means that many different target languages can be used. In all these systems, the efforts of a skilled human is still needed to complete the translation. What the current generation of translation machines does is reduce the work involved in human translation (Hillenbrand 1989, p. 62).

Recognition

Speech recognition and speech synthesis

Computers that can receive input and give output using voice would make a major difference to the way we use computers. The interfaces that are difficult to interact with, the need for accurate typing, would all but disappear. If only computers could accept and use natural voice language, we might witness a breakthrough in hand-held computers, often called personal computerized or digital assistants. Already we have the technology for miniaturization, but current technology is restricted because input has to be via a keyboard (or mouse) or using text, icons, or digits only. Keyboards prevent very small hand-held devices from being made. Digits or other icon systems are limited in the number of items that can be input. For example, a hand-held icon device works well to take orders in a restaurant, which has a limited set of items. It would not work well for wordprocessing or information retrieval. Already, in many parts of the world, people hear synthetically produced words. When calling directory assistance in the United States, the caller commonly hears the number produced synthetically. To use natural language voice, computers need to 'hear' natural language, process the grammar (discussed above under parsers), and then produce speech.

SPEECH RECOGNITION
Computer scientists refer to this step as 'recognition' rather than 'understanding' because the latter not only implies intelligence but also knowledge of the world. Speech recognition, then, is a model of discernment of sounds. To recognize natural speech computers need to train on huge amounts of data (which is becoming more and more possible with high-speed computing) and, more impor-

tantly, search for meaningful patterns in a sea of irrelevant sounds and noises. For speech recognition to become viable in any but small domains, the system must be speaker accent independent (that is, capable of recognizing speech from any voice) and be able to untangle continuous speech.

In the early 1980s, isolated, whole-word recognition systems were the most successful, using a technique known as dynamic warping, which is a template matching procedure; more recently, the technique of hidden Markov modelling is used, which extracts probabalistic information about speech units, but requires a vast amount of training data in order for the system to 'learn' how to recognize speech segments. Speech recognition systems convert the acoustic signal into digital form, extract the meaningful sounds, and then classify the meaningful sounds. Clearly, extracting meaningful sounds while rejecting background noise is difficult. But, even more difficult, is the classification or identification of the meaningful sounds. One approach attempts to match the incoming sound with a 'dictionary' of stored prototypical sounds. This approach only works in applications that are limited, requiring only a small number of dictionary entries. The more matches that need to be made, the more processing the computer needs to do. The computer needs to store vast amounts of data and also takes time to find the match. Thus, it works for single-word recognition such as a code for entry into a building, but not for continuous speech. A second approach is to analyse sounds into their constituent features, such as pitch and timing. Again, pattern matching is employed. But, the amount of data that has to be stored is limited since it is restricted to features, not the individual pronunciation of an infinite number of sounds and words. A third approach includes syntactic and semantic processing. Either information is analysed at one level and then passed onto the next level of language, or information is passed among the levels, trying to find the level which has the best solution for the current identification problem.

Common to all these approaches are several still unsolved problems. How can the system determine regularities from variation? Even individual speech sounds (phonemes) vary according to their context. So, for example, the acoustic properties of the 't' in 'toe' are different from the acoustic properties of the 't' in 'stow'. The sounds also vary across speakers due to dialect variation or individual voice quality. The other major hindrance is the recognition of continuous speech, with its slurs and unmarked boundaries between words. The matching techniques that work moderately well for single-word recognition are very inaccurate (often around 60 per cent accuracy) in identifying words in continuous speech.

Until these problems are solved, speech recognition systems will be of use only in restricted domains such as voice activated appliances, or responding to one speaker's voice, with a limited context-dependent vocabulary. While linguists and others continue to work on these problems, the general public will continue to interact with computers via keyboards, mice and other devices. It is therefore imperative that research into human–computer interaction continue, with the goal of making computers accessible (and usable) to all people. We can not afford to wait for breakthroughs in speech recognition.

SPEECH SYNTHESIS

For HAL and C3P0 to become reality, we need machines that not only recognize human speech but also respond with speech that humans can understand. However, 'speech synthesis', which refers to the electronic creation of speech, is a model only of articulation not of speaking. Speaking requires language understanding.

The earliest speech synthesis systems simply selected and played back pre-recorded (and digitized) words and phrases. This process was used in many directory assistance programs. Although the result was flat and unnatural, lacking the intonation and rhythms of human speech, it was clear and adequate for simple applications like articulating numbers. Later speech synthesis systems took the individual sounds of English, electronically reproduced their acoustic properties and reassembled the sounds in a particular word. The next step was to analyse words for their acoustic properties and follow the same basic procedure. But, such systems are limited to individual words, the individual words being strung together to form utterances. Most of us have heard these disem-bodied voices – they sound synthetic and often are unrecognizable to humans. Progress has been made with the current generation of chip-level digital signal processors. Most personal computers can be equipped at moderate cost with circuitry capable of producing reasonably intelligible speech from computer text. Many of the natural rhythms, intonation and stress of human speech are reproduced, albeit rigidly (for example, the '.' symbol generates a falling tone). Although the speech is instantly recognizable as being artificial and *not* human, these systems are adequate for many purposes and have proven to be very valuable to the sight impaired. These speech generation devices are driven by the internal computer representation of text, such as that with which a wordprocessor works. How then do computers work with the common human forms of text representation – print and hand-writing? The next section deals with this issue.

Image recognition

If we cannot talk to our computer, perhaps we can write to it. One thing that most living creatures do extremely well, and machines do very poorly, is to process visual information, including reading. The state of the art in image recognition and processing by machines might be acceptable for terrain following missiles and smart bombs, but it would be foolish to allow a self-guiding vehicle on an empty country road, to say nothing of trusting to it a bus load of school children during freeway rush hour.

But let us return to our main theme and the more limited domain of machine recognition of written language. Again we find that the results are very mixed, with some success in limited domains and essentially complete failure at the text understanding level.

Inexpensive scanners and PC software are capable of converting some forms of printed text to computer text. Programs can also receive fax transmissions and convert print images to text. But even the most sophisticated systems are limited in the fonts they can recognize and they are easily confused by varying fonts and type sizes occurring in the same document as well as the introduction of images, boxed text, tables, multi-column formats and other features of printed matter that humans handle with no difficulty.

One of the most successful applications of text recognition has been machines that scan printed text and, using speech synthesis, 'read' the text to the sight impaired. The translation from printed text to speech is not perfect, for example when the program encounters new words it spells them letter by letter, and the speech is clearly machine-like. But such machines liberate the sight impaired from dependency on a sighted reader.

It has proven impossible to convert print reliably to computer text; it is even more difficult to program a computer to recognize handwriting. Nevertheless, some machines on the market do accept handwritten material as input. Some of these machines and programs work from scanned input, others use special screens or styluses to transfer the handwritten image into the computer. Computers without keyboards, relying totally on writing and pointing with a pen or stylus, have just come on the market as this book is published. The overall accuracy of these machines is not high. The best results are achieved when printing is used (block capitals work best) and after a period of 'training' the machine to recognize the idiosyncracies of an individual hand. The recognition of cursive handwriting is much less successful although the research is definitely hopeful (Brocklehurst, 1988).

The limited, but real, successes in the recognition of human written text have primarily been with Western alphabetic languages. The emphasis has been on recognition, not on the cognitive aspects of understanding what has been written. Two of the primary objectives of the Japanese 'fifth generation project' (Feigenbaum and McCorduck, 1983) were in natural language processing and image processing. These ambitions were at least partially based on a need to recognize and manipulate the Japanese written language. Written Japanese is extremely difficult, consisting of three forms (katakana, hiragana and kanji), most commonly used in combination, one of which (kanji) is Chinese pictographic. To complicate matters further, a romanized script (-romanji) is also employed, punctuation is far from standardized, western numerals and forms are intermixed and writing may be from left to right, top to bottom **or** top to bottom, right to left. The analysis of Unger (1987) would clearly (and correctly) lead one to expect that the 'fifth generation project' would fail to meet its language processing goals. The claims that the Japanese are over 90 per cent literate are exaggerated. Many more years of more intensive schooling are required to reach an equivalent level of fluency compared to Western alphabetic languages and college level is required for complete mastery. It does appear that a very high form of human cognitive ability is needed to read and write Japanese fluently and so it is not surprising that the machine recognition and processing of that language has met with small success.

World knowledge

Even if the computer could be programmed to process natural language, how could it deal with the following?

Read the following story and answer the question below:
Susan went to a restaurant.
   She ordered a hamburger.
   She paid the cashier and left the restaurant.
Question: What did Susan eat?

A relatively small child can answer this question. But for a computer to answer it, it must have background knowledge about what happens in restaurants – that we order something we want to eat and usually eat it. Schank and Abelson (1977) used scripts to encode information about such everyday situations. But, these scripts have severe limitations – they are linear and so the information can only be processed in the same sequence as in the script. So, for example, as happens at the *Sizzler* chain of restaurants, if you pay the cashier before being seated and eating, the script could not process a scenario such as

Susan went to a restaurant. She sat down. She got mad and left.

Further, how does the system know which scripts to apply to which scenarios?
   Scripts are but one approach to the general problem of knowledge representation. Once the knowledge in a particular domain has been represented, there is the question of how the computer can reason, using that knowledge and human language.

How intelligent are computers?

Even if voice recognition and speech synthesis systems become viable and computers have a knowledge base, they are not understanding and speaking systems. How then can computers be programmed to understand? This is the crux of the artificial intelligence debate. First, we need to ask the criteria by which we will decide that a computer system is intelligent. Once we know that, we can then examine whether computers can perform, measuring up to those criteria.
   The most often used criterion is the one referred to earlier, the Turing Test – that a third party can not distinguish between the behaviour of a human and a machine. This does not, of course,

imply the machine must be an android. The test can be keyboard input and screen output at a computer terminal, where in one case the responder is human, and in the other case the responder is a computer program. John Searle (1980) posed an example – the Chinese Room – that indirectly argues against the Turing Test.

Imagine that you (a non-Chinese speaker) are locked in a room with only one entrance and one exit. Chinese symbols come into the room through the entrance and other symbols leave via the exit. You have a book of instructions in English, that tells you to send certain symbols out the exit as certain other symbols come in through the entrance. If you follow the instructions, anyone outside the room could think that you speak and understand Chinese. The analogy to the computer is that the characters coming into the room are input while those going out are output and your book of instructions is a program. No matter how impressive your performance, it can not be said that you understand Chinese.

Still, the strong version of AI claims that machines can be programmed to replicate the same reasoning processes as humans. Fundamental to this belief is the assumption that we understand human reasoning, and even more importantly, that human reasoning is a logical, rule-governed process. Thus, many AI researchers such as Herbert Simon work on the assumption that human intelligence is largely a matter of problem solving. If those problem-solving procedures can be made explicit, they can be written into mathematical formalisms. Such a view ignores many other aspects of human intelligent behaviour, such as intuition.

Games

Nevertheless, this view of intelligence as problem-solving plus the Turing Test as a discriminator has led both sides of the AI argument to focus on games as a means of demonstrating machine intelligence, or the lack of it. The trivial games, like tic-tac-toe, fell early and easily to the 'superiority' of the machine – machines play these games perfectly. That was a trivial demonstration, so attention moved to more complex games, like blackjack and checkers, and machines triumphed again (although a computer has yet to defeat consistently the world chequers champion). The battlefield shifted to chess, oft cited as the highest form of human cognitive endeavour in microcosm. Despite early difficulties (chess is quite a difficult game), chess programs now play at grand master level and only the very best human players are capable of defeating them. Chess programs will soon be unbeatable and effort is already shifting to the Japanese game of Go.

The Dreyfus brothers (1986) argue that computer game programs, specifically chess, utilize processes that are at best similar to those used by merely competent players and not at all like those used by human experts. Their arguments are compelling and certainly relevant in a broader context which we will explore later. But this is beside the point where games are concerned. Games are very limited domains and are inherently governed by relatively simple rules which are innately subject to programming (sophisticated programming, perhaps, but programming none the less). With sufficient computational power, the machine will ultimately win. That alone does not determine intelligence and perhaps a better test is whether a machine can create a popular game rather than whether it can win.

Heuristics

No-one denies that computers can simulate many functions of human reasoning, such as number crunching. But, do they replicate human reasoning processes? Computers operate by manipulating numbers (and numbers can represent symbols), using algorithms. Algorithms are procedures with a finite number of steps for solving a problem for which there is a precise solution. But much of human reasoning has neither a single solution nor a simple process. For such problems, AI researchers employ an heuristic approach, finding a solution that is good enough, but not necessarily the best. The process then involves generating many potential solutions and comparing them with the goal. In other words, a trial and error method, where a new rule is added whenever a case is found that is not handled by the original rules. One of the disadvantages is that the user does not know what new rules the program is adding to its store, leading to unpredictable results.

Expert systems

'Expert' systems, 'knowledge based' systems – these are compelling terms, not chosen by accident, evoking images of the tireless guru with the immediate answer to difficult problems. These are diagnosticians and teachers, engineers and executives, technicians and public servants, stock brokers and generals always on call and able to provide quickly the very best advice and generate the correct decision.

An expert system is a computer program tailored to a specific application, like the quality control of a manufactured part or the diagnosis of lung disease. It receives as input a set of facts – measurements or observations – often from a menu or via pre-programmed questions or in machine readable form produced by other machines and instruments. The system then analyses these observations using a set of programmed rules and key values of the observed quantities (the knowledge base). This analysis is really a set of (more or less) complex 'if x then y else z' manipulations. The consequence of this analysis is the system's decision. Some expert systems can provide a summary of the salient branches in this decision tree thus 'explaining' how they reached their conclusions. Others produce a list of possible solutions with associated probabilities. Expert systems can be programmed to ask follow-up questions in order to obtain more information on which to refine their judgements.

This simplified description is not intended to trivialize the issue for these are often highly complex systems capable of handling wide variations, even uncertainties, in their domains of input. The ultimate goal is to mimic the ability that the true expert in a given field has, which is to reach sound judgements and conclusions in situations which she has not experienced before.

The key element of an expert system is the knowledge base – the distilled wisdom of a human expert in the field. The fundamental assumption of the knowledge base is that the masters of a skill develop, with experience over time, vast knowledge of facts about the skill plus rules for interrelating observations of situations and deriving conclusions. The 'facts' sought for the knowledge base are not limited to textbook cases or tables of numbers, but include as much as possible of what the expert has personally experienced. The 'rules' are not limited to the purely analytical (mathematical formulae or physical laws), but include the insights and 'rules of thumb' that the true expert always seems to generate. Eliciting this knowledge from the expert and coding it into the knowledge base is far from easy and has given rise to the new profession of 'knowledge engineering'. The knowledge engineer works by interviewing experts in the task being modelled to find out how they make their judgements. Computer programs have been developed to make the job of building the expert system easier (expert system shells). However, obtaining the *information* for the knowledge base is a tedious, iterative task frequently frustrating to both the knowledge engineer and the expert. With those requirements, it would appear that the best knowledge engineer is a combination of psychologist and programmer and it probably would help to have a good grasp of the field of the expert being interviewed. Perhaps the best knowledge engineer of all would be an expert in the task being modelled who also has expertise in building knowledge-based systems.

There have been many useful applications of expert system technology in industry and elsewhere – there are expert system-based chess programs, medical diagnostic programs, computer configators, chemical analysts, engine diagnostic systems, plant schedulers, and so on. Specialized expert systems and expert system shell programs have been commercially available for several years on a variety of computer platforms from PC size up. Why then are expert systems not pervasive and why, after all this time, have they not had the impact predicted by their proponents (see for example Feigenbaum and McCorduck, 1983, Feigenbaum, et al. 1988)? Where are the expert machine diagnosticians, teachers, executives and generals that we looked for in the introduction to this section? Even the concerns of Dreyfus and Dreyfus (1986, p. 121) that '[t]o the extent that junior employees using expert systems come to see expertise as a function of large knowledge bases and masses of inferential rules, they will fail to progress beyond the competent level of their machines' have failed to materialize.

The answer, well articulated in Dreyfus and Dreyfus, is that these are not *expert* systems at all, but are at best merely *competent*. These programs do not reproduce the problem-solving processes of a human expert and rarely, if ever, achieve the success rate of the human experts upon whose knowledge they are based. The tediousness and frustration of the knowledge engineering process must serve as a warning – human experts, when required, *will* articulate rules for how they reach their judgements, but then acknowledge that is not how they reach conclusions when exercising their expertise. The terms and phrases most commonly used to describe the process – 'feel', 'intuition', 'I did this once before and it worked', etc., etc. – do nothing to describe how a human being thinks, whether it be writing, conversing or running an assembly line. Whatever that process is, it is not how computers or computer programs ('expert' systems or otherwise) work. Like most other

Fetzer (1990) explores the philosophical foundations of AI from the perspective of the theory of knowledge. Obermeier (1989) presents a concise, but thorough overview of *Natural Language Processing Technologies in Artificial Intelligence: The Science and Industry Perspective*. Boden (1977) presents an early history of AI. Winograd's 1984 article in *Scientific American* is still the most accessible account of the difficulties of programming computers to use natural language.

EIGHT

Public highway or private road? or Who is in charge?

This chapter, based on the uses of information technology discussed in the previous chapters, addresses what are essentially issues of public policy and social ethics, rather than questions of the technology itself. Computers have made information more widely available, allowed for the rapid retrieval of data, selection and matching of data from different sources, and the rapid analysis of data. Many commentators and researchers agree with Tom Peters, who, in the Foreword to *The Rise of the Expert Company* (Feigenbaum et al. 1988), claims that

> The world of organizing human activities is undergoing its first genuine revolution since the correctly labeled industrial 'revolution' of the late eighteenth century. The information-processing technologies that are empowering the new revolution may eventually have more impact on human organization – public and private – than did the mass production revolution, powered first by steam.
>
> (Feigenbaum et al. 1988, p. vii)

The terms and metaphors used to describe the new technology lead us to ignore the social context in which the technology is introduced. These metaphors and terms take on a positive, progressive stance. Computer technology is a revolution, is transformative, is liberating, will make us more productive, will create a global village. What it hides is the historical fact that the introduction of all new technologies (from the stylus to the printed book to the spinning jenny) is not socially or morally neutral. The technology may be socially and morally neutral (some commentators would even dispute that claim), but its introduction is not. The printing press, for example, made information more widely available, but did not, in and of itself, lead to the reformation (as some claim). Rather, the seeds of the reformation were already well in place; the technology allowed current thinking to be expressed and distributed. In

Chapter 2, I discussed more fully this parallel with the introduction of the computer. Thus, any changes brought about by the computer are likely to reflect current values, hence the computer metaphors that focus on productivity. Despite these positive metaphors, if we look at questions of public policy and social ethics, rather than at how much data a computer can store or process, we find the exact same tensions that exist in our society at large – tensions among privacy, security, freedom, access, and control.

I have used the metaphor of a highway as the title to this chapter because as I write (early 1994), the Information Superhighway is a focal point of discussion and technological direction. Newspapers, presidents, scholars and shop-assistants are all fascinated by the notion of unlimited access to information and communications. However, this metaphor also invokes the ethical issues – Who will build the highway? Who will pay for its construction? Who will have access to it? Will it be a toll road or a freeway? Will travel be restricted, controlled? What will the rules of the road be like? Who will police it? What, if any, on-ramps will there be? This chapter will problematize the issues underlying these questions, issues that primarily revolve around two human rights – the right to complete and accurate information and the right to keep some information private.

The use of the highway metaphor also makes information tech-nology appear benign. By choosing a known, accepted metaphor, we can gloss over some of the essential characteristics of informa-tion technology, characteristics that have the potential for both good and bad. Computer technology is highly complex, as any of us who have learned to use a new system or have experienced fail-ure in computer software or hardware know. Most people choose not to become experts, preferring to use the technology much like their toaster. When is does not work, we call someone in to fix it. We therefore leave ourselves in the hands of a profession that, so far, has limited self-regulatory practices. The Internet was once a community of tightly knit academics and scientists with a shared social consensus and, therefore, informal rules of conduct. Now that it has burgeoned into a world of 20 million people, the same destructive and deviant behaviour found in the real world is found in the virtual one. Most of the professional organizations such as ACM (Association of Computing Machinery) have developed ethi-cal standards which they ask their members to adhere to. But, unlike medicine, with its disciplinary hearings and de-certification, there is no unified code of enforceable ethics. Additionally, because it is complex, computer technology is vulnerable – to poor design, to lack of control and to malicious intent. And, too, because computer use is so widespread and so many essential societal functions (such as hospitals, banks, water supplies) depend on them, the potential for social disaster is great. Make books available to ordinary people and you hasten the advance of the reformation; make networked computer systems available to terrorists and you could bring entire cities and countries into chaos, as suggested by futurist Alvin Toffler in his most recent book, *War and Anti-War* (1992). These information technology characteristics and their attendant effects on our social lives must be addressed by computer professionals, the lay public and politicians. They are not only questions of technology, but also raise questions of social values and ethics. These values and ethics can be divided into four issues: 1) ownership of information, 2) responsibility for the content of information, 3) freedom of speech and information, and 4) the right to privacy. In problematizing these issues, more questions than answers are raised, primarily because these are ethical issues, ones that must be decided by society at large and individuals within society.

OWNERSHIP OF INFORMATION

Software

There is probably no reader who has not at some time, wittingly or unwittingly, used a computer program that was pirated. It is so easy to copy software – certainly easier than copying a complete printed book, as easy as copying a record or CD onto a tape. People often do not accept that they have pirated (as the software industry calls it) the software, claiming that the companies make large profits, or it is not really like stealing because it is a copy – the original still exists. Many software companies claim that for every one copy they sell, two more are made illicitly. Recent estimates in the United States are that the value of pirated software is around US$1 billion and could easily be 10 times that amount world-wide. Companies have tried various solutions, including making it impossible to copy the disk, but that means the owner can not make a back-up copy, essential because of the problem of damage. Other solutions include providing a password in the hard copy manual (usually people only copy the disk, not the manual), but users find it annoying. Since 1993, the Software Publishers Association has distributed a videotape to schools, an eight-minute rap telling kids 'Don't copy the floppy' (Kanaley, 1994, 4F).

Over the centuries since the printing press made reproduction of intellectual ideas simpler, Western nations have developed copyright and patent laws that protect ideas. Ideas are property in the West, an extension of our homes, cars and other possessions. Many other cultures do not have a tradition of intellectual property rights; instead, ideas are part of the common culture. The history of copyright and patent is embedded in the United States Constitution, which seeks to promote the progress of ideas by protecting them. Progress is taken to mean diversity, not the protection of the rights of the inventor. Current print copyright laws are inadequate for software; similarly, current patent laws are inadequate. Copyright applies to an intellectual work such as print or possibly a computer program; patents are granted for 17 years (in the United States) to ideas that result in devices or the implementation of a program, in addition to the devices themselves. Software differs from the types of devices usually granted patents: it has many components; independent invention of the same technique is common; many equivalent procedures can be used to achieve the same purpose; similar procedures can be used for different purposes. And, as the chairman of Wind River Systems says, 'In a field changing as fast as software is today, 17 years might as well be a millenium. The deal might as well be phrased, "Tell us your idea, and you can monopolize it forever"'(Glass, 1994, 1E).

To copyright or patent software, we have to ask what exactly constitutes the program. Different legal cases have argued for the source code, the algorithms, structure, and, more recently, the 'look and feel,' of a program. Borland was successfully sued by Lotus because its spreadsheet program, Quattro Pro, used the same command structure as that of Lotus 1-2-3. Operations in Quattro Pro looked like that of Lotus 1-2-3 *and*, more importantly, used the same underlying program structure. Using only the 'look and feel' argument, Apple unsuccessfully sued Microsoft for its Windows program, claiming that it had the look and feel of the Macintosh interface and so was protected. Apple, meanwhile, was sued by Xerox for its use of the mouse and icons, both invented at Xerox. Xerox lost the case, not on the grounds of ownership, but because, by the time the case was heard, it had already exceeded the validity time for patents. A recent court decision has awarded a small Southern Californian software developer, Stac Electronics, $120 million in damages because Microsoft's data compression utility in its latest MS-DOS 6 infringed on their patent. In this case, Microsoft used Stac's methodology without a licensing agreement.

Some form of protection is needed if companies are to invest in innovation and develop new products. Yet, the protection can not be so great that they have a monopoly on what may in fact be a natural progression in software development. Many changes in software are incremental, such as the interface. If copyrighted, only the owner can make those incremental changes and the owner is not likely to want to change if his interface is the *de facto* standard. Any other inventor or company wishing to write a software program compatible with others (e.g., for use on the Macintosh interface) would have to make it much like currently available software, which would be illegal. Also, strong patents or copyright or trade secret laws would make it difficult, if not impossible, for researchers to move to another job in another company. How can they not take their ideas and knowledge with them? Thus, software and patents tend to protect the status quo.

Documents

The question of intellectual property was also raised earlier in relation to writing that appears in electronic form. In print form it is protected by current copyright laws. But what about an electronic version? United States copyright law has so far claimed that it is intellectual property and covered by 'literary works' copyright. But, we have seen that electronic texts are infinitely malleable and can be changed by others. At what point of change does the original author no longer have copyright? How can (or even should) writers protect their information from being used? Currently, research performed by academics usually results in ownership over the work they produce, either through patent or copyright. But, more and more faculty members are being encouraged to use instructional media or multi-media. Many lectures are delivered via multimedia. Thus, the lecture can be recorded and stored electronically. Who owns the lecture? The faculty member who developed it? Or the university that provided and owns the multi-media? Many of these questions will need to be answered through court precedent and legislation. However, property ownership affects us all. All information technology users pay more for their software to help defray litigation costs. Software prices are high because companies know it will be copied and they will not have the maximum profit because the product can not be distributed by them as much as possible; so each item carries an individual higher price. And, it is not only the professionals who have intellectual property. As more and more people are connected through networks, all of us will exchange ideas and information. Do we want those ideas and information to be acknowledged as ours? If we do, how should such acknowledgements be made?

This latter question also raises the issue of who should have access to information – not just software. Who decides? If the information is mine, do I decide or does the company or organization on whose network the information resides make the decision? Law courts in Britain and Australia have ruled that ideas are not property. Their logic is this: if someone steals your idea, you still have the idea and so it is not stolen. But, British law says that prying into someone's computer is trespass. Yet, other countries do not have such a law. So, people in countries such as Japan or Australia, which do not have such laws, can pry into British computers with impunity. They can not be prosecuted in their own countries or extradited because there is no such law in their countries.

So, is our hacker who uncovers covert operations by a government a hero or a criminal? How much privacy should the individual expect? Before addressing these related issues, we need to examine who is liable for the accuracy of the information. Having it owned by someone is not sufficient. For the information to be useable, it must be reliable; yet computer software and hardware are prone to breakdowns which can cause either a complete inability to access information or the distribution of inaccurate information.

RESPONSIBILITY FOR THE CONTENT OF INFORMATION

In January 1990, one of AT&T's (the major US long-distance telephone company) computers thought it was overloaded and rejected calls. In minutes, the 114 back-up computers across the US tried to take the excess calls only to also find themselves overloaded and so rejected the calls. Callers from all over the world, trying to call the US, heard only recorded messages stating that all circuits were busy. Only 50% of the 148 million calls placed actually succeeded. Mastercard, which processes 200,000 credit card approvals each day could not process them.

American Airlines Reservation Agents could not make bookings, despite their sophisticated monitoring and reservation system. Hotel and car rental companies could not make reservations. Chaos continued for nine hours.

(Elmer-Dewitt 1990, pp. 58–9)

No, this was not a terrorist attack, nor was it a virus or worm planted by some hacker. The error was a 'bug' in the computer program. Who is responsible for the subsequent loss of business? AT&T? The programmers? Computer software programs for many operations consist of millions of lines of code, written by a team of programmers who know only about the small section of code for which they are responsible. Only when the whole is put together do many of the problems surface. Only when certain routines and operations occur in certain ways do some of the 'bugs' become noticeable. Like many weapons systems, most computer programs can not be tested, except in the 'marketplace' for which they were designed. Simulations used to test the programs are only that – simulations. It is just not feasible to test all the permutations and combinations possible in such complex programs – that would take longer than our lives. Consequently, most software does not come with warranties, but with disclaimers as to liability. '[W]e are forced to acknowledge that the construction of software is a complex and difficult process and that existing techniques do not provide software of assured quality and reliability' (Forester and Morrison 1990, p. 83).

The AT&T example is only one of thousands of computer breakdowns, many of which have been life-threatening. A United States Space Shuttle launch was aborted because of computer glitches – the program produced the wrong combination of sequences. In 1989 a bug shut down Tokyo's Dai-Ichi Kangyo Bank's 1,800 automated tellers. In 1989 American Airlines reservation system went down, forcing agents to book flights by hand. A misprogrammed medical X-ray machine delivered excess doses of radium to several cancer patients, killing one and paralysing others. In 1980, the United States Strategic Air Command System displayed Soviet intercontinental ballistic missiles heading towards the USA – but it was a false alert. A similar incident occurred a few days later. Investigation found a faulty computer chip. We have all read of the telephone bills for millions of dollars, or the interference from former President Reagan's plane that caused garage door openers to malfunction, or the hundreds of other errors in our lives that have been explained as the computer's fault.

Not all failures are related to errors in the software code. Some are the result of a faulty system and/or interface design that leads to human error. The USS *Vincennes* shot down an Iranian civilian airliner when the crew misinterpreted the ship's computer display. Although the immediate error was attributable to human misinterpretation, the error was the result of poor display design. As I have discussed earlier in Chapter 3, the gulf between the abstract functions of the computer and the tasks the user wants to perform makes it more difficult for the user to intuitively determine what to do next or how to overcome an error. Norman (1988) suggests that to remedy this situation, programmers need to work with experts on human behavior to develop interfaces that are more logical to the average user.

Other failures are the result of poor maintenance of databases.

I first became aware of my death last May when my checks began to bounce. Never having experienced bouncing checks before, and knowing that I had quite a respectable balance in the bank, I was both shocked and angry. When I examined the returned checks and found, stamped over my signature on each of them, in red ink, 'Deceased', I was mystified. Then, when one of the recipients of my checks, a utility company, demanded that I appear in person, cash in hand, plus $10 for their trouble – *their* trouble – I was shocked, angry and mystified. I wondered just how they expected us deceased to acquiesce.

(Brown as reported by Forester and Morrison 1990, pp. 75–6)

Brown also experienced problems with his Social Security check and Medicare – his doctor did not receive payment for treating him because he had 'died' six months earlier. These latter problems resulted from the wrong information of his death being shared among several different databases – his bank and government healthcare and government pension. I will deal later in this chapter with this issue of matching data across different systems. Here, the issue is the possible unreliability of the information held in databases.

Society is still left with the ethical dilemma of who (if anyone) should take responsibility for computer failures. Imagine an expert system designed to read lung X-rays, but which fails to diagnose lung cancer in a patient who subsequently dies. Who is responsible?

Is the expert at fault for not providing enough 'expertise?' Even doctors reading X-rays themselves miss important cues or misread. Is the knowledge engineer at fault for not eliciting enough expertise? Can the knowledge engineer know when she has enough information? Is the programmer (or programmers) at fault for not translating the knowledge into impeccable code? Is the company at fault for developing an interface the doctor can easily misinterpret? Is the company at fault for not testing the software in all its infinite permutations and combinations? Is the doctor who relies on the expert system at fault for assuming the software decisions were accurate? Is the patient at fault for accepting the doctor's information? Should the patient even have the expectation that the diagnosis will be correct, given the limitations of both computer technology and medical science? There are no easy answers to these questions. But, society must engage in the debate about the ethical liability of computer failure, neither accepting failure as 'the computer's fault' nor assuming computers are infallible.

Another instance of responsibility is the accuracy or truth of the information. A recent case in Australia highlights this issue. An anthropologist at the University of Western Australia is alleging defamation by e-mail. As discussed in the chapter on Computer-mediated Communication (CmC), questions of etiquette and ethics have constantly been raised concerning the content of bulletin boards and e-mail. But, this is the first case of defamation. Most commentators claim that current laws relating to print, radio and television media will apply. But, because of a lack of security, e-mail is different. Although unlikely, it is possible that the author of the scurrilous e-mail was not the person whose name appeared on the e-mail. Expert network users know how to use another person's log-on and ID, just as the German spy did. In addition, is the network legally liable? Or is the university whose system originated the message? Network experts think not. The tradition in print is that the publisher is liable. But, in electronic form, who exactly is the publisher? Cases such as this have not yet reached the courts. In the meantime, some people call for censorship and/or surveillance by employers.

FREEDOM OF SPEECH

Using information technology, what rights do individuals and groups have to publish their ideas? Freedom of speech is enshrined in the constitutions, precedents, and laws of most democracies and the limits to that freedom using traditional media such as print and television have been established through years of legislative or court deliberation. Decisions are either to control what is said or control who has access. So, in the USA, publishers may publish pornographic material, but it can not be sold to minors; nor can minors participate in the production of the material (as actors, for example). Already we have seen pornography on bulletin boards. Is this socially acceptable? I will address this issue from the two sides – controlling what people can say and controlling who has access to information.

Censorship

Although the question of censorship applies to all electronically produced information, bulletin boards are a typical example of the issues. Most conferences and bulletin boards have moderators who decide what should and should not be included – both in terms of content and tone. But, does anyone else have the right to censor CmC? Currently, CmC does not fall under any censorship guidelines in any country that I know of. Several recent cases raised the whole issue of censorship. The first involved Prodigy, a 1,500,000 member online information system owned jointly by Sears and IBM, the second, Stanford University. When Prodigy decided to raise its fees, subscribers began posting messages on the bulletin board, protesting. Prodigy officials responded by banning the discussion of the topic in public (online) forums. Protestors who then protested using the more private e-mail were removed from the network.

The Stanford case involved jokes. Through networks, users in universities and companies have access to a file of jokes, as well as other information on using the UNIX operating system. The jokes were typed in by Brad Templeton in Ontario, Canada. He rejected the most scurrilous, encrypted ones that might offend, and coded for possible offensiveness such as 'race', 'sex', 'gross' and, for ethnic jokes, substituted a meaningless acronym for the name of the group. However, he failed to code one racist joke and this resulted in a heated exchange in bulletin board messages about the appropriateness of racist and sexist jokes. This exchange came to the notice of Stanford officials when a lower-level computer worker mentioned it. Stanford then began blocking access to the jokes file, on the grounds that the jokes 'undermine an important university purpose: our collective search for a better way for a truly pluralistic community in which every person is acknowledged an individual, not a caricature'. Officials were especially inclined to prevent access since it is merely a file and does not include a forum where the issues raised by the jokes can be discussed. For many computer professionals and others, Stanford's reaction was considered equivalent to the Vatican's index of prohibited books during the middle ages. For them, the question is not the suitability of the joke, but, as John McCarthy, Professor of Computer Science says, that 'we consider it contrary to the function of a university to censor the presence of newsgroups [bulletin boards] in university computers ... To be able to read anything subject only to cost limitations is an essential part of academic freedom' (Harper 1989, p. 10A).

Yet, calls for control are frequent, especially concerning the content of bulletin boards. As mentioned earlier, when the Internet was the province of a small group of scientists and academics with their own shared code of conduct, censorship was rarely raised. But, since it has become a world network of 20 million users, what some consider abuses have proliferated. One group, calling itself AST (based on the initials of their electronic address) is committed to inciting abusive exchanges, as they state in their manifesto. They target special interest groups, such as pet owners, and send them graphic messages about cat killing. They have posed as outraged puritans on an erotic newsgroup. They claim it is a prank. Yet, many receivers of their e-mail have felt threatened.

Other more disturbing cases involve children who have 'met' adults electronically, only to find they are paedophiles, who send sexually explicit material to children or young people. Parents need to be aware of such possibilities. They are certainly aware of violence and explicit sex on television and, depending on the family values, choose what their children can and can not watch. The same needs to hold for electronic information. A recent *San José Mercury News* article (Eickmann 1994, 1H, 5H) provided a list of 'rules' for children using online services, summarized below:

1. Warn children to never send personal information.
2. Do not allow children to go online unsupervised if they are not old enough to go out to public places unsupervised.
3. Make the password difficult to crack. Tell children to protect it.

4. Check whether the online service allows parents to block certain features.
5. Tell them about unpleasant situations they may encounter and teach them strategies for handling them.
6. Teach children not to engage in inappropriate behaviour themselves (e.g., cursing).

Two recent cases on the Internet are ironic. Many Internet users have supported groups even as anti-social as AST on the basis of freedom of speech – that the electronic world should remain as unrestricted as it has always been, with people loosely agreeing to unwritten norms of 'netiquette'. Recently, however, their notion of freedom of speech has been tested by two Phoenix lawyers who posted on a bulletin board an offer to help people seeking work or immigration permits. 'No advertising on Internet!' shouted Internet's most ardent proponents of free speech. In fact, the two lawyers were mail bombed, their electronic mail box (and their fax and telephone lines) becoming clogged with virulent messages, messages that were abusive and defamatory.

Also, in February 1994, the commercial online service, America Online automatically subscribed its members to longstanding Internet newsgroups. 'This is serious! It's like hell has been released! Our relatively quiet country roads are being changed into smoking, flat asphalt buzzing with ... AOLites' (Plotnikoff 1994, 1C) flamed one longtime newsgroup participant. The incident mirrors any cultural clash, as newcomers try to learn the conventions of the host culture. Since the netiquette of the Internet is unwritten, it takes time for new users to learn the cultural literacy. America Online users were used to a network that offers service-for-fee, that has people in charge; the Internet is unregulated, free and traditionally collaborative. America Online users, like novice e-mail users I studied, are often verbose, asking long-winded questions, with politeness markers, about elementary concepts. Internet users expect short, to-the-point, direct and new questions. New users take up discourse threads that have long since gone out of debate. Old users keep track of the multiple discourse threads in the newsgroups, remembering what is old and new information. New users often post decontextualized notes such as 'me too' or 'I agree', with no reference to the concept or note to which it is a response. These two examples illustrate the dilemma between giving access to all (see discussion below) to speak freely and how to manage the access and what people say. It is ironic that the very (formerly exclusive) club built on freedom and even anarchy is the first to complain about others having the same privileges.

Commercial online services (e.g., Prodigy) believe they have the right to control what is sent, just as television networks control what is broadcast. In the latter case, however, government also controls, setting standards and ratings, assigning certain types of programs to certain times. These rules have been worked out over time, using government legislation, lobbying from special interest groups, and court cases. Online services are only just coming into the public arena and so no consensus has been reached. However, it is vital that computer professionals, governments, and the general public begin discussion, especially since Internet has grown and the United States government is advocating access to the Information Superhighway for all.

Access to information

Given that the information can be faulty because of human or machine errors or may contain socially unacceptable material (e.g., pornography directed towards children), the issue arises as to who has the right to what information. Some cases seem clear and covered by current social values and laws concerning property. For example, when a bank clerk uses her knowledge of the computer system to skim money from many users' accounts, depositing the money in her own account in Switzerland, a crime of theft has clearly been committed. These types of computer crimes have increased rapidly, largely because the opportunity presents itself more easily. It is certainly easier, and less dangerous, to use Electronic Funds Transfer (EFT) to commit a crime than to hold up a bank with a gun. Hearnden (1989) found that most computer crime is committed by employees, from clerks and cashiers to management. The employee who alters inventories and redirects some items to himself and then sells them, is also clearly committing a crime of theft. But what about copying a computer program? Or what if someone changes information in a computer? Or what if it is a 14 year-old from New York City, who takes over the operations of remote computer systems, making them into bulletin boards for his friends to play on (Elmer-Dewitt 1991, p. 81)? Or what if someone uses information gained from a database for personal or political benefit? What if it is the government that accesses the information?

Businesses and governments that advocate strong control over who has access to information often do so because they are concerned that information will 'get into the wrong hands' or people with malicious intent will destroy their information and profits.

Hackers

A hacker in Hanover, Germany, calls a public access modem, hooks into a 'Datex-P' network, connects to a personal computer in the library of the University of Bremen, and disconnects the accounting system so that the library pays for the telephone bills to connect to the U.S. Once gaining access to the U.S., he breaks into the computer at Mitre Corp., a defense contractor near Washington D.C., uses their modems (and they consequently are billed for the outgoing phone calls) to connect to Tymnet, connects with the Lawrence Berkeley National Laboratory and uses their computers as the illicit gateway to Milnet and Arpanet, networks that link the military, defense contractors, research laboratories and universities. He then exchanges the secrets he discovers for cash and cocaine.

(Stober 1989, p. 7B)

The term hacker was first used to describe computer software writers who tried to understand the entire workings of a computer system – people who could almost build their own computers – and some did. Even today, many of these aging hackers meet together for conferences where their discussions range from highly technical ones about programming codes to the hardware, to ethical issues. Their intent was never malicious damage, but rather a desire to exhibit their cleverness and skill at programming and their understanding of the operating systems themselves. These hackers shared programs and ideas and a common love for the aesthetics of computers. According to Levy (1985), who wrote *Hackers: Heroes of the Computer Revolution*, this approach changed when software was commercialized. Such hackers still exist. But, the term's everyday use, especially in the media, usually refers to someone who maliciously manipulates the computer or creates a scam. These people need extraordinary knowledge of systems and programming, as in the case of the German spy discussed at the beginning of the section. And such knowledge can be used to disastrous effect given that most commercial and government computers are connected via the Internet.

Network systems expand the vulnerability of computers, as

evidenced by two headline events in 1989 – the network worm let loose by the Cornell student and the break-in by the German spy. Both events have been widely documented in the media and in a book written by Clifford Stoll (1989) on how he tracked his German hacker. The German spy story illustrates one of the social issues that accompanies CmC. The German intruder attacked 450 computers and succeeded in accessing about 30, at army bases, defence contractors, and a nuclear weapons laboratory. Stoll's two-year odyssey began when he noticed a 50-cent billing discrepancy for computer time at Lawrence Berkeley National Laboratory. He found that someone had created a fictional user on the system, without a corresponding billing account. The hacker found a back door into computers by becoming system manager or super-user, both of whom have special status on computer systems, being able to look around to see if anyone was watching him. The hacker then turned off the accounting so that there was no trace of his break-in or activities. Through the Lawrence Berkeley computers, the hacker was able to access defence computers on MILNET and ARPANET. He was able to use legitimate accounts because, using his super-user status, he could search for passwords and userids. His searches were helped by sloppy users who sent passwords to friends via e-mail or stored their passwords in files. For encrypted passwords, he ran a program on his own computer in Germany that compared the encrypted passwords with the encrypted form of every word in the English dictionary. Once inside systems and with a legitimate account, the hacker searched for sensitive data such as on NORAD (an air attack warning/defence system). And all the time he was logged on to US computers via tortuous routes over telephone lines, he did not even pay for the phone calls – he established billing at his first entry system in the US so that that organization footed the bill!

Bulletin boards, too, have suffered from the malicious tricks played by some hackers. Some hackers crash the bulletin board itself. Others post an innocent-looking program, that turns out to be a worm or virus, programs that infiltrate systems and do damage, such as wiping out an entire hard disk. These types of behaviours are largely the result of the ability to be anonymous, to exercise power over people and machines, with the belief that the hacker will not be found out – and the vulnerability of computer systems. In this way, such computer crashing and break-in is no different from vandalism or burglary.

Yet, many innocent people have been caught in the fall-out from hacking. The United States Secret Service mounted Operation Sun Devil to break up a ring of hackers called the Legion of Doom. Mostly in their teens and early twenties, these hackers, who went by code names such as Acid Phreak and The Prophet, had downloaded a telephone company document that detailed the administrative procedures for their emergency telephone system. They posted it on a bulletin board and subsequently it was picked up by others. One hundred and fifty Operation Sun Devil agents then raided the homes of many bulletin board contributors who had been in contact with the Legion of Doom, which was not a formal group with known membership. Even the members themselves did not know how many members there were. One of many innocent people caught in the operation was a small computer games company, the owner of which had, unbeknown to him, hired a former Legion of Doom member. Consequently, the Secret Service confiscated his computers and hard and floppy disks, claiming he was about to produce an electronic game that would be a handbook on computer crime. He thus lost business, laying off more than half his employees (reported by John Barlow in *The CPSR Newsletter*, 1990, pp. 1–18). The allegation of a computer crime handbook has never been proven. Dozens of bulletin boards that had copies of the document were closed down by the agents, bulletin boards that may be as protected by the United States Constitution as any book or magazine. Where was their right to publish? Interpretations of the Fourth Amendment to the United States Constitution already have claimed that government can not seize printing presses or typewriters, to prevent them from publishing anything that is protected free speech. But, no such interpretations exist for electronic files. Now, a computer is often the printing press, typesetter, and filing cabinet.

One solution, of course, is to prevent crime, tighten computer security, using, for example, encryption devices, or access-control software. The former scramble information so that only the person with the key can decode the encrypted information. Since almost all codes can eventually be broken, they need to be changed often, which adds to the expense. The latter either restrict users to only those files they are authorized to use or have a dial-back password check. Neither prevents employee crime from those with legitimate access. In addition to the technical problems of security are questions of values. Many in the computer industry, and especially the hackers, roamed in a free cyberspace before computers became popular. They had no need of security or controls. Many of them knew each other, even if only electronically. They developed a sense of community and trust. For them, the controls suggested by management and government are antithetical to the whole culture of information technology as they see it.

As with the introduction of all new media initially, the law is ambiguous. Old rules do not always apply to new forms and functions. Many government agencies want strong controls to protect society from the potential chaos that can be caused by the unauthorized access to computer systems. Civil liberties groups and many computer professionals want to maintain the freedom that has allowed the free range of ideas and data, resulting in the development of the new technology. What is essential as societies work out ways to prevent crime, is that they still maintain the rights of individuals. Control of systems used to prevent crime can equally be used for surveillance.

Authorized access

So far, we have looked only at access that could be construed as illegal. But, an even more important issue is who has legal access to the Information Superhighway. Although the media and others talk of the computer revolution, whose revolution is it? Although there were 59 million PCs in use in the United States in 1990, according to Mulgan (1991), most demands for information technology come from industry, government and the military. Further, the technology that is in schools and homes is in the schools and homes of the richest sectors of society. The ideal envisioned by those who promote the Information Superhighway is a free flow of information, a society in which any individual can call up the information they need for work and leisure, from wherever they happen to be. In our homes, we can choose among hundreds of television channels; we can call up our favourite symphony from a central database and it will be piped right into our homes; we can call up our favourite book from the library, read it online, hear it read to us, or order it and have it delivered from the library; we can check that reference or historical fact that we can not quite remember. What is rarely discussed is who the 'we' is. If the development of the superhighway is a joint government/industry endeavour, who pays for what services? Will it be like the telephone, where the user pays? Or will it be like the freeway, where all can use it – subject to buying and maintaining a car, of course? And, it is more than a question of access. Information is not valuable in and of itself. Its power and ours lie in our ability to *use* information. A standing joke in most countries is the VCR that blinks 12:00. The controls and commands for VCR machines are so complex that many people use them only for viewing a rented video from a store – not for recording shows. The information available on the superhighway must be useable by all. As we have seen, current implementations of the technology require literacy skills as well as technical skills. Unless all have access and can use it, the superhighway will maintain the status quo. Those with the money, the education and the literacy will be able to access and use the information; those without will become even further disenfranchised.

PRIVACY

Many CmC users are lulled into a sense of false security – that their system is invulnerable and that they have final control over their messages. During the Iran-Contra investigation and hearings, Oliver North found, to his dismay, that he had not had complete control over his message system. Like many universities, government agencies and businesses, the CmC system used at the White House during North's year of Contra fund raising was PROFS (an IBM e-mail, document, and calendaring system standing for Professional Office System). North shredded most hard copy documents, and thought he had deleted all his soft copy documents. Reports differ as to how his deleted memos were retrieved. Some claim he had, in fact, used the 'delete' command; but, unbeknown to him (and many other users), this command merely erases the file label, leaving the text itself in an electronic limbo from which it can be recovered by system programmers. Others claim that the system programmers backed up data frequently to tape, a common and desirable practice in any organization or home. In either event, congressional investigators were able to search the disks (or tapes) and recover critical documents that revealed North's involvement in raising money for the Contras.

Employer surveillance

While many are grateful that North was exposed, others, such as civil liberties groups claim that any access to hidden files, and so forth should only occur with a court order and when the investigators are sure a crime has been committed. They oppose any routine access by employers. Yet, it is precisely the ability to recover deleted PC files that allows commercial packages to recover many lost files and files deleted in error – if they are searched for before they have been overwritten. And, it is the back-up practice of system programmers that has allowed many computer users to 'find' files they had accidentally erased. In either case, what we see here is a change in the nature of text permanency. Although, as I have discussed when talking about literacy, electronic text is fluid, malleable and impermanent, it can be less erasable than paper text, unless we take special precautions. Programs do exist that allow encryption of data and also the overwriting of files so that no previously recorded electronic data are retrievable.

Information technology, as we saw in the case of sales agents at American Airlines, makes it easy for employers to monitor the work of employees, counting keystrokes, listening in to conversations with customers, checking on bathroom breaks and so on. And, this is no isolated case. A 1993 survey by MacWorld found that 21 per cent of their respondents had searched employees computer files and 12 per cent considered monitoring to evaluate worker performance was acceptable (Flynn 1993, p. 3F). This issue is a conflict between the individual's right to privacy and the employer's right to know what workers are doing with company equipment. In the United States, a 1986 federal law extended a former law that prevented a third party from tapping telephone lines to include those used for e-mail; but that law does not cover employers monitoring employees. In various courtcases, employers have been granted the right to monitor employee's use of telephones and inter-office mail. As I write, several cases are pending, ones that examine whether employers have the right to access employees' e-mail.

The next several years should see further examination of this issue. 'The protection of personal privacy in the information age may be as crucial for American workers as the protection of safety was in the age of machines' (Rotenberg 1993, p. 4). To this end, the MacWorld report included a model privacy policy including the following:

- Employees should know what electronic surveillance tools are used, and how management will use the data gathered.

- Management should minimize electronic monitoring as much as possible. Continuous monitoring should not be permitted.
- Data should only be used for clearly defined, work-related purposes.
- Management should not engage in secret monitoring unless there is credible evidence of criminal activity or serious wrong-doing.
- Data gathered through monitoring should not be the sole factor in employee evaluations.
- Personal information gathered by employers should not be disclosed to any third parties, except to comply with legal requirements.
- Employees or prospective employees should not be asked to waive privacy rights.
- Managers who violate these privacy principles should be subject to discipline or termination.

(Rotenberg 1993, pp. 5–6)

Institutional surveillance

In late 1990, Lotus Development Corp. announced a joint venture with Equifax, a credit-rating bureau. Their plan was to sell a PC product, called 'Marketplace Households', with information on the shopping habits of U.S. households. When the joint venture was announced, 30,000 people called, asking that their names be removed from the database. People were concerned with security, privacy, and the 'opt-out' option. Without any other discussion, the project was canceled in January 1991.

(Elmer-Dewitt 1991, p. 81)

The government of Thailand, in an effort to computerize the nation's social services, will, by 2006, have vital data on its 65 million inhabitants on a single, integrated computer network. The data include name, age, education, family history, tax status and criminal record. Integrated systems such as this have been denied in most industrialized countries. In the United States, for example, data collected by one government department for a particular purpose (for example, the census), can not be used for another purpose (for example, taxation). These controls have been enshrined in law and legal decisions to ensure some measure of privacy of individual citizens from a possible Big Brother government. British law allows individuals to access information that others hold about them. To put teeth into this, the law requires that people holding personal data must register it in the Data Register. However, the registration process is cumbersomely bureaucratic. Yet, what is considered private varies across cultures. The United States credit information companies collect data that would be an invasion of privacy in Germany; yet Germans report their change of address to the police while Americans would consider this an invasion of privacy. When United States telephone companies began offering Caller ID (a system that displays the number of the caller, even if they have an unlisted number), many people objected, claiming invasion of privacy. Consequently, several states passed laws requiring companies to offer customers the choice of blocking their numbers from being displayed. In other countries, however, governments have used databases precisely to monitor citizens. South Africa, in its apartheid days, used computer systems to enforce travel restrictions on the black population.

The conflict here is between the right to obtain information and the right to withhold some information. Most Western democracies give governments rights to information that might be criminal. In the case of Operation Sun Devil, federal agents had the right to investigate and seize property if they had obtained permission from a judge who had decided there was sufficient evidence that a crime had been committed. In addition, most Western democracies give citizens the right to information about government decisions. Even highly sensitive data can be released after a period of time. This right, hard won by civil liberties' groups, is to ensure that governments do not carry on with activities that its citizenry would not approve of. The right to withhold information is the right to privacy. Clearly, there is always a delicate balance between privacy and the right to information.

Prior to electronic storage and retrieval of data, time and technology were on the side of privacy. If a government agency wanted information about you, it would have to consult paper files. If a different agency wanted that information, they would have to try to get it from the agency holding the data. What is different now, is that linked databases can share and match information; record-keeping is simpler and less expensive; greater quantities of data can be stored over longer time periods. In the case of Brown (who had 'deceased') above, the erroneous information that he had died was shared among three different agencies, two government and one a private bank. Yet, most people would be pleased if banks gave information to police agencies so an escaped killer is apprehended. But, when we apply for a home loan, do we want the bank to have access to our medical records from our physician? When we are admitted to emergency after a car accident, do we want the hospital to have access to information about our bank balances or our mortgage payments from our bank, or about our travel habits from our travel agent? These are not idle questions. Banks may want to find out if we can afford the repayments on the loan. Hospitals may want to find out if we can afford to pay for the treatment. But, these databases have made our lives easier. It is only because they hold financial data about us that we can use EFT at banks or even our credit cards. As mentioned earlier, the American Express expert system can gauge whether the purchase is legitimate, based on our previous transactions. It is the matching of data from one system to another that seems to infringe on our privacy because the individual has lost control of who has the data and for what purposes. A mailing list is neutral, but not when tied to income, crime statistics, ethnicity and medical history. A potential solution is laws such as those in Britain that maintain a registry of databases and allow access to individuals of information held on them; yet even such systems are difficult to enforce.

These ethical and social issues are not so much technical questions, but a continuing societal discussion about who has what information, for what purposes. Ironically, the very technology that allows data matching also allows us to audit, to check who has accessed what information.

How well we allow this marvelous invention to continue to be developed by creative minds, while we seek to prohibit or discourage truly abusive practices, will depend upon the degree of wisdom that guides our courts, our legislatures, and governmental agencies entrusted with authority in this area of our national life.

(Barlow 1990, p. 18)

FOR DISCUSSION

1. To what extent should the privacy of individuals be violated in order to protect other individuals? What should be the limits and constraints placed on organizations who hold data on individuals?

2. Are hackers criminals? What activities mentioned here do you consider to be crimes?
3. Should software be copyrighted or patented? Why?
4. Who should be held legally responsible for computer failures? Why?

FOR ACTION

1. Interview a manager in a company or government office and ask what security measures they use to prevent unauthorized access to their computer data. Assess these measures for their adequacy to protect both individuals and the organization's data.
2. Research what laws have been passed in your country concerning access to data held on individuals.
3. Imagine you are the manager in a large bank that has the ability to monitor employees, holds financial data on its customers, and could have access to regional medical records online. Develop your own Information Age Privacy Protection Rules for this company – rules for management, employees and customers. Provide a rationale for your rules.

FURTHER READING

Denning (1990) provides a detailed set of readings on unauthorized access to computers and its legal, social, and ethical implications. Norman (1988) discusses the non-intuitiveness of much technology, including computers. Forester and Morrison (1990) discuss the ethical issues computer professionals need to address. CPSR (Computer Professional for Social Responsibility) produces documents and newsletters that discuss the issues in this chapter.

Glossary

AI	artificial intelligence. A field with the goal of getting machines to perform high level intelligent functions of humans, such as speech, problem solving, etc.
algorithm	Procedure with a finite number of steps for solving a problem.
America Online	Online service providing e-mail, bulletin boards, travel, shopping, financial services, news, games. Membership primarily in the United States and Canada.
ARPANET	Advanced Research Projects Agency Network. Starting in 1969, a network of computers linking defence contractors and defence-related research institutions in the United States, subsequently developed into the Internet.
ASCII	American National Standard Code for Information Interchange. An internationally recognized standard code for representing numbers, letters of the alphabet, special characters (e.g. currency symbols) and some other common symbols in binary (bits).
ATM	Automatic teller machine. An electronic terminal and machine where people can transfer funds, withdraw or deposit money to/from their bank.
bit	Binary digIT. Number system consisting of zeros (0) and ones (1). For example, two (2) is represented as '10' (one, zero).
BITNET	BITNET (Because It's Time Network). A computer network of, primarily, academic institutions. Connected, through gateways, to the Internet.
bug	An error in a computer program that causes it to malfunction.
Bulletin board	An online service where users can 'post' messages that can be read by anyone who has access to the service.
caller ID	A telephone service that allows the callee to see a display of the telephone number of the caller.
CD ROM	Abbreviation for Compact Disk, Read Only

	Memory. A disk for storing large amounts of data. Users can access the data but can not write on the disk.
chat room	Online interaction in real-time among several people all connected to the online service. Chat rooms are usually devoted to specific topics.
CmC	Abbreviation for computer-mediated communication. Any communication sent and received electronically.
code	Euphemism for computer program (as in 'this program consists of some many million lines of code').
CompuServe	One of the oldest (started in 1970) online services providing e-mail, databases, bulletin boards, shopping, airline reservations, stock quotations, etc.
computer chips	The basic hardware components of a computer (the central processor, memory, etc.).
CPSR	Abbreviation for Computer Professionals for Social Responsibility. A US-based association that monitors the use and abuse of computers in industry and government.
cracker	A person who illicitly penetrates and subverts computer systems.
crash	Computer failure. Usually referring to a software failure.
cyber	Derived from cybernetics, the study of control functions and computers. Often used as a prefix as in 'cyber-space'.
database	Information stored electronically in a structured, retrievable form.
Delphi	Online service targeted at home and corporate users, offering e-mail, bulletin boards, databases.
digital	Organizing data by representing them as two types of signals – 0 and 1.
domain	Specific area of knowledge.
download/upload	To move information from another computer to one's own computer (down) or from one's own computer to another (up).
EFT	Abbreviation for Electronic Funds Transfer. Transfer of money electronically (e.g. from one bank account to another).
EIES	Abbreviation for Electronic Information Exchange System. One of the first conferencing systems. Not widely used or known.
e-mail	Messages written on a computer, sent electronically and received by another computer. E-mail can be stored for future reference.
emoticon	Icon used to indicate emotion e.g., :>)
encryption	Coding/scrambling of data to make it unreadable until decoded with a secret key.

expert system	An AI program that performs specialized tasks by using a body of knowledge about the tasks.
fax (Machine)	Abbreviation for facsimile transmission (x-mission). A machine that accepts printed matter and sends it via standard telephone lines to another machine which converts it back to printed matter on paper.
flaming	Emotional exchanges of insult and abuse sent electronically.
GEnie	General Electric Network Information Exchange. A home user-orientated online service, offering e-mail, bulletin boards and databases.
hacker	Computer expert who enjoys exploring and developing computer systems and tinkering for fun. Now most commonly used in association with illicit activities (see cracker, above).
hard copy	Text or graphics printed on paper.
hardware	The computer and its various parts.
heuristic	Experiential knowledge.
hypertext	Software that allows the user to write text that branches and links in many different directions.
ID/userid	A name, number, or combination of both that uniquely identifies a user on a computer. The combination of userid and computer ID identifies the person on the network.
Information Superway	Official name National Information Infra-structure. A network envisaged by the Clinton Administration, that would link all Americans electronically offering connection to entertainment, shopping, databases, e-mail, bulletin boards.
interface	What the user sees on the computer screen, designed to simplify the interaction between the person and the computer.
Internet	Created in the 1970s as a United States Defense Department research and development project to electronically link selected computers involved in defence research (government, corporations and universities). It now links hundreds of other networks. It is loosely organized and free-wheeling.
knowledge base	The wisdom of a human expert in a field distilled into an AI (expert system) computer program.
Knowledge engineer	Person who designs and builds expert systems.
LAN	Abbreviation for Local Area Network. A network linking computers that are close to each other (usually within a few hundred metres of a central point, e.g. a single building or floor).
log on/off	To connect to or disconnect from a computer/userid.

mail bomb	Large volumes of unsolicited e-mail sent to opponents, clogging their electronic mailboxes.
MCI Mail	An online service of MCI Corporation offering e-mail, bulletin boards, databases, fax, etc.
menu	List of options the user can choose from.
modem	Hardware device for converting a computer's digital signals into a form suitable for transmission across standard telephone lines.
Minitel Services Co.	A French-based online service, offering e-mail, bulletin boards, databases and shopping. Based on a specially designed (Videotex) terminal.
NII	National Information Infrastructure, popularly known as the Information Superhighway.
newsgroups	Electronic bulletin boards devoted to specific topics, where users can 'post' notices that will be read (and responded to) by other users.
password	A (usually) self-selected secret string of characters used to identify an individual and give them access to a computer service.
PC	Abbreviation for personal computer. An individual computer designed for home or office use.
piracy	Copying software without permission of the author.
Prodigy	An on-line service targeted at the home user and small office, offering e-mail, bulletin boards, shopping, games, airline reservations and databases.
shell	Computer software package that has many of the programs necessary for building an expert system. Knowledge engineers use the shell to construct specific programs for specific domains.
smiley	Icon to convey emotion e.g., :>)
soft copy	Text or graphics stored electronically.
software	Computer program.
sneakernet	A play on words referring to the practice of 'transmitting' data from one place to another by putting it on a floppy disk and carrying it to another person/machine.
stand-alone computer	A computer that can work by itself, not needing another computer to function. Can be networked to other machines.
terminal	A display screen with keyboard that is connected to a computer. Usually large computers (mainframes, minis) have many terminals connected to them and many people can be using the same machine at the same time.
The Source	An online service targeted at business and financial researchers.
Turing Test	Named after computer scientist Alan Turing. The test is that if a machine's behaviour is

	indistinguishable from that of a human, then the machine is intelligent.
virtual	As in virtual reality or virtual machine. A simulation.
virus	A computer program that inserts itself into programs on other computers and disks each time the infected program is executed. Most viruses affect the basic system that operates the computer and are usually very destructive to data on the computer.
VNET	Virtual Network. The network that links all IBM facilities worldwide.
voice mail	Telephone service that allows callers to leave messages that the callee can later listen to.
wordprocessing	Software that allows the user to enter text, manipulate it electronically, and prepare it for printing.
worm	A form of virus propagated through networks.

SOFTWARE PACKAGES CITED

ELIZA	Program designed to perform like a humanistic counsellor.
Gopher	A tool developed at the University of Minnesota to help find information on the Internet.
Lotus 1-2-3	Spreadsheet program, product of Lotus Development Corporation.
Meteo	Machine translation program translating English weather forecasts into French.
MS-DOS	Microsoft Disk Operating System. The underlying program that runs most IBM-compatible personal computers.
Note Bene	Wordprocessing program for academics, the product of Dragon Fly Software Corporation.
PROFS	Abbreviation for Professional Office System. An IBM package for e-mail, document handling and calendaring, available on IBM mainframe and mini-computers.
Quattro Pro	Spreadsheet program, product of Borland International Incorporated.
RightWriter	Style-checker.
Unix	The underlying program (operating system) that runs many large computers, mini-computers and workstations (the most powerful personal computers). Originally developed at the AT&T Bell Laboratories, now existing in many versions.
Windows	Graphical user interface on personal computers. A product of Microsoft Corporation.

Writer's Helper   Style-checker, a product of Conduit.

Writer's Workbench   Style-checker,   developed   by   AT&T/Bell
                         Laboratories.

Writing to Read   IBM integrated program for teaching young chil-
                         dren to read through writing using computers.

References

Abramson, J. B., Arterton, F. C. and Orren, G. R. (1988) *The Electronic Commonwealth: The Impact of Media Technologies on Democratic Politics.* New York: Basic Books.

Arkin, M. and Gallagher, B. (1984) Word processing and the basic writer. *Connecticut English Journal,* 15, 2, 60–6.

Balestri, D. P. (1988) Softcopy and hard: wordprocessing and writing process. *Academic Computing,* February 14–45.

Barlow, J. P. (1990) Crime and puzzlement. *The CPSR Newsletter,* Fall, 1–18.

Bell, P. and Stern, J. (1994) NII in education: access isn't enough. *The CPSR Newsletter,* Spring, 4–5.

Boden, M. A. (1977) *Artificial Intelligence and Natural Man.* New York: Basic Books.

Bolter, J. D. (1989) Beyond word processing: the computer as a new writing space. *Language and Communication,* 9, 2/3, 129–42.

Boyd, R. S. (1994) Survey finds many Americans have low interest in high-tech. *San José Mercury News,* 8 May, 9A.

Brecher, D. (1985) *The Women's Computer Literacy Handbook.* New York: New American Library.

Brocklehurst, E. R. (1988) *The NPL Electronic Paper Project* (NPL Report, DITC 133/88). Teddington, Middlesex: National Physical Laboratory.

Brod, C. (1984) *Technostress: The Human Cost of the Computer Revolution.* Reading, Mass: Addison-Wesley.

Brown, S., Levin, J., Mehan, H. and Quinn, C. (1983) Real time interaction: unraveling multiple threads of discourse. *Discourse Processes,* 6, 59–75.

Buchwald, A. (1988) Cancel the war: our computer's down. *San José Mercury News,* 31 March, 10E.

Burns, H. and Culp, G. (1980) Stimulating invention in English composition through computer-mediated instruction. *English Technology,* August, 5–10.

Case, D. (1985) Processing professional words: Personal computers and the writing habits of university professors. *College Composition and Communication,* 36, 3, 317–322.

Catano, J. (1985) Navigating the fluid text. *College Composition and Communication,* 36, 3, 309–316.

Chafe, W. L. (1982) Integration and involvement in speaking, writing, and oral literature. In D. Tannen (ed.), *Spoken and Written Language: Exploring Orality and Literacy* . Norwood, NJ: Ablex, pp. 35–53.

Chaiklin, S. and Lewis, M. W. (1988) Will there be teachers in the classroom of the future? . . . But we don't think about that. In R. D. McClintock (eds.), *Computing and education: The Second Frontier*. New York: Teachers College Press, pp. 80–89.

Collier, R. (1983) The word processor and revision strategies. *College Composition and Communication*, 34, 149–55

Cross, G. (1990) Left to their own devices: three basic writers using word processing. *Computers and Composition*, 7, 2, 47–58.

Cuffaro, H. K. (1984) Microcomputers in education: Why is earlier better? In D. Sloan (eds.), *The Computer in Education: A Critical Perspective*. New York: Teachers College Press.

Daiute, C. (1985) *Writing and computers*. Reading, Mass.: Addison-Wesley.

Daiute, C. (1986) Physical and cognitive factors in revising: Insights from studies with computers. *Research in the Teaching of English*, 20, 2, 141–59.

Davis, F. E. (1987) Desk-top publishing means fewer academics will perish. *San José Mercury News.*, 22 November, 1F and 8F.

DeMott, B. (1990) Why we read and write. *Educational Leadership*, March, 6.

Denning, P. J. (ed.) (1990) *Computers Under Attack: Intruders, Worms and Viruses*. Reading, Mass.: Addison-Wesley.

DeVillar, R. A. and Faltis, C. J. (1991) *Computers and Cultural Diversity: Restructuring for School Success*. Albany, NY: State University of New York Press.

Dobrin, D. N. (1987) Some ideas about idea processors. In L. Gerrard (eds), *Writing at Century's End*. New York: Random House, pp. 95–107.

Dreyfus, H. L. and Dreyfus, S. E. (1986) *Mind Over Machine*. New York: The Free Press.

Dubin, F. (1987) Answering machines. *English Today*, April, 28–30.

Duranti, A. (1986) Framing discourse in a new medium: openings in electronic mail. *Quarterly Newsletter of the Laboratory of Comparative Human Cognition*, 8, 64–81.

Eickmann, L. (1994) Virtual parenting. *San José Mercury News*, 20 March, 1H, 5H.

Eisenstein, E. (1979) *Communications and Cultural Transformations in Early-modern Europe*, Volume 1, *The printing press as an agent of change*. New York: Cambridge University Press.

Ellis, R. (1985) *Understanding Second Language Acquisition*. Oxford: Oxford University Press.

Elmer-Dewitt, P. (1990) Ghost in the machine. *Time*, 29 January, 58–59.

Elmer-Dewitt, P. (1991) Cyberpunks and the constitution. *Time*, 8 April, 58–9.

Elmer-Dewitt, P. (1994) Who should keep the keys. *Time*, 14 March, 90–1.

Feigenbaum, E. and McCorduck, P. (1983) *The Fifth Generation: Artificial Intelligence and Japan's Computer Challenge to the World*. New York: Signet.

Feigenbaum, E., McCorduck, P. and Nii, H. P. (1988) *The Rise of the Expert Company*. New York: Time Books.

Ferguson, C. (1977) Baby talk as simplified register. In C. Snow and C. Ferguson (eds), *Talking to Children*. Cambridge: Cambridge University Press, pp. 209–35.

Ferrara, K., Brunner, H. and Whittemore, G. (1991) Interactive written discourse as an emergent register. *Written Communication*, 8, 1, 8–34.

Fetzer, J. H. (1990) *Artificial Intelligence: Its Scope and Limits*. Dordrecht: Kluwer Academic Publishers.

First, S. E. (1988) Putting E-mail to work. *PC World*, March, 210–13.

Firth, J. (1957) *Papers in Linguistics 1934–1951*. London: Oxford University Press.

Flores, F., Graves, M., Hartfield, B. and Winograd, T. (1988) Computer systems and the design of organizational interaction. *ACM Transactions on Office Information Systems*, 6, 2, 153–72.

Flower, L. (1979) Writer-based prose: a cognitive basis for problems in writing. *College English*, 41, 1, 19–38.

Flynn, L. (1993) They're watching you. *San José Mercury News*, 13 June, 1F and 5F.

Forester, T. and Morrison, P. (1990) *Computer Ethics: Cautionary Tales and Ethical Dilemmas in Computing*. Oxford: Basil Blackwell.

Friedrich, O. (1983) The computer moves in. *Time*, 3 January, 4–24.

Gaies, S. (1977) The nature of linguistic input in formal second language learning: linguistic and communicative strategies in ESL teachers' classroom language. In H. Brown, R. Crymes and C. Yorio (eds), *On TESOL '77*. Washington, DC: TESOL, pp. 204–12.

Gargan, E. A. (1994) Towering over Babel. *San José Mercury News*, 29 May, 1E, 7E.

Garson, B. (1988) *The Electronic Sweatshop*. New York: Simon and Schuster.

Gerrard, L. (ed.) (1987) *Writing at Century's End: Essays on Computer-Aided Composition*. New York: Random House.

Gibbs, M. and Smith, R. (1993) *Navigating the Internet*. Indianapolis, IN: Sams Publishing.

Glass, B. (1994) Creative licenses. *San José Mercury News*, 24 April, 1E, 9E.

Goodman, P. S., Sproull, L. S. and Associates (1990) *Technology and Organizations*. San Francisco: Jossey-Bass.

Goody, J. and Watt, I. (1968) The consequences of literacy. In J. Goody (eds), *Literacy in Traditional Societies*. Cambridge: Cambridge University Press, pp. 53–84.

Granbard, S. R. (ed.) (1988) *The Artificial Intelligence Debate*. Boston, Mass.: MIT Press.

Greene, B. (1983) Electronic mail: personal touch destined for doom? *San José Mercury News*, 23 October.

Greenfield, P. M. (1984) *The Effects of Television, Video Games, and Computers*. Cambridge, Mass.: Harvard University Press.

Grice, H. (1975) Logic and conversation. In P. Cole and J. Morgan (eds), *Syntax and semantics*, Volume 3: *Speech acts*. New York: Academic Press, pp. 41–58.

Grow, G. (1988) Lessons from the computer writing problems of professionals. *College Composition and Communication*, 39, 2, 217–20.

Halliday, M. (1978) *Language as Social Semiotic*. London: Edward Arnold.

Halliday, M. A. K. (1985) *Spoken and Written Language*. Burwood, Victoria: Deakin University Press.

Halpern, J. and Liggett, S. (1985) *Computers and Composing*. Carbondale, Ill.: Southern Illinois University Press.

Harasim, L. M. (ed.) (1990) *Online Education: Perspectives on a New Environment*. New York: Praeger.

Harper, P. (1989) Not book burning, but close. *San José Mercury News*, 6 February, 10A.

Harris, J. (1985) Student writers and word processing: a preliminary evaluation. *College Composition and Communication*, 36, 3, 323–331.

Hartman, K., Neuwirth, C. M., Kiesler, S., Sproull, L., Cochran, C., Palmquist, M. and Zubrow, D. (1991) Patterns of social interaction and learning to write: some effects of network technologies. *Written Communication*, 8, 1, 79–113.

Havelock, E. (1982) *The Literate Revolution in Greece and its Cultural Consequences*. Princeton: Princeton University Press.

Havelock, E. A. (1963) *Preface to Plato*. Cambridge, Mass.: Harvard University Press.

Hawisher, G. E. and Selfe, C. L. (eds) (1991) *Evolving Perspectives on Computers and Composition Studies: Questions for the 1990s*. Urbana, Ill.: NCTE.

Heap, J. L. (1989) Collaborative practices during word processing in a first grade classroom. In C. Emihovich (ed.), *Locating Learning: Ethnographic Perspectives on Classroom Research*. Norwood, N.J.: Ablex.

Hearnden, K. (1989) Computer criminals are human, too. In T. Forester (ed), *Computers in the Human Context*. Oxford: Basil Blackwell, pp. 415–42.

Heath, S. B. (1983) *Ways with Words*. Cambridge: Cambridge University Press.

Heath, S. B. and Hoffman, D. (1986) *Interactive Reading and Writing in Elementary Classrooms* [Guidebook for inside learners (film)].

Heim, M. (1987) *Electric Language: A Philosophical Study of Word Processing*. New Haven: Yale University Press.

Henzl, V. (1974) Linguistic register of foreign language instruction. *Language Learning*, 23, 437–454.

Hillenbrand, B. (1989) Trying to decipher Babel. *Time*, 24 July, 62.

Hiltz, S. R. (1984) *Online Communities: A Case Study of the Office of the Future*. Norwood, NJ: Ablex.

Hiltz, S. R. and Turoff, M. (1978) *The Network Nation: Human Communication via Computer*. Reading, Mass.: Addison-Wesley.

Hollis, R. (1984) REAL executives don't use computers. *San José Mercury News*, 15 April, 1F, 14F.

Holzman, M. (1989) Nominal and active literacy. In M. M. Cooper and M. Holzman (eds), *Writing as Social Action*. Portsmouth, NH: Boynton/Cook, pp. 157–73.

Howard, R. (1985) *Brave New Workplace*. New York: Viking.

Hunt, P. and Vassiliadis, K. (1988) No easy answers: investigating computer error messages. In S. Doheny-Farina (ed.), *Effective Documentation: What we have Learned from Research*. Cambridge, Mass.: The MIT Press, pp. 127–42.

Hymes, D. (1972a) Models of the interaction of language and social life. In J. Gumperz and D. Hymes (eds), *Directions in Sociolinguistics*. New York: Holt, Rinehart & Winston, pp. 35–71.

Hymes, D. (1972b) The scope of sociolinguistics. In R. W. Shuy (ed.), *Sociolinguistics: Current Trends and Prospects*. Washington, DC: Georgetown University Press, pp. 313–33.

Janda, R. D. (1985) Note-taking English as a simplified register. *Discourse Processes*, 8, 4, 437–54.

Johnson, B. M. and Rice, D. E. (1987) *Managing Organizations Innovation: The Evolution from Word Processing to Office Information Systems*. New York: Columbia University Press.

Just, A. M. and Carpenter, P. A. (1980) A theory of reading: from eye fixation to comprehension. *Psycholinguistics*, 87, 329–54.

Kanaley, R. (1994) The $100 million loophole. *San José Mercury News*, 10 April, 1F, 4F.

Kaplan, R. B. (1966) Cultural thought patterns in intercultural education. *Language Learning*, 16, 1–20.

Kaplan, R. B. (ed.) (1983) *Annual Review of Applied Linguistics*. Reading, Mass.: Addison-Wesley.

Kelly, E. and Raleigh, D. (1990) Integrating word processing skills with revision skills. *Computers and the Humanities*, 24, 1/2, 5–13.

Kerr, E. B. and Hiltz, S. R. (1982) *Computer-Mediated Communication Systems*. New York: Academic Press.

Kiesler, S., Siegel, J. and McGuire, T. W. (1984) Social psychological aspects of computer-mediated communication. *American Psychologist*, 38, 1123–34.

Kintsch, W. (1988) The role of knowledge in discourse comprehension: a construction-integration model. *Psychological Review*, 95, 163–82.

Kirkman, J. (1980) *Good Style for Scientific and Engineering Writing*. London: Pitman.

Kleifgen, J. (1991) Kreyol ekri; kreyol li: Haitian children and computers. *Educational Horizons*, 69, 3, 152–8.

Lakoff, G. and Johnson, M. (1980) *Metaphors We Live By*. Chicago, Ill.: University of Chicago Press.

Laver, M. (1975) *Computers, Communications and Society*. London: Oxford University Press.

Leech, G. (1966) *English in Advertising*. London: Longman.

Levinson, S. C. (1983) *Pragmatics*. Cambridge: Cambridge University Press.

Levy, S. (1985) *Hackers: Heroes of the Computer Revolution*. New York: Doubleday.

Longley, D. and Shain, M. (1984) *The Microcomputer User's Handbook*. New York: John Wiley and Sons.

Lyman, P. (1994) Cyberspace as campus: how will information technology change teaching and learning? presentation, San José State University, 17 February.

Malinowski, B. (1923) The problem of meaning in primitive languages. In C. Ogden and I. Richards (eds.), *The Meaning of Meaning*. London: Kegan Paul.

March, J. G. and Sproull, L. S. (1990) Technology, management and competitive advantage. In P. S. Goodman, L. S. Sproull and Associates (eds), *Technology and Organizations*. San Francisco: Jossey-Bass, pp. 144–73.

Markus, M. L. (1988a) Electronic mail as the medium of managerial choice. *Information Systems Working Paper*. The John E. Anderson Graduate School of Management at UCLA, pp. 4–89.

Markus, M. L. (1988b) Asynchronous tools in face-to-face groups. *Information Systems Working Paper*. The John E. Anderson Graduate School of Management at UCLA, pp. 3–89.

McClintock, R. O. (ed.) (1988) *Computing and Education: The Second Frontier*. New York: Teachers College Press.

McCorduck, P. (1985) *The Universal Machine*. New York: McGraw-Hill.

McLuhan, M. (1962) *The Gutenberg Galaxy: The Making of Typographic Man*. Toronto: University of Toronto Press.

McLuhan, M. (1964) *Understanding Media: The Extension of Man*. New York: McGraw-Hill.

Mulgan, G. (1991) *Communication and Control*. New York: Guilford Press.

Murray, D. E. (1985) Composition as conversation: the computer terminal as medium of communication. In L. Odell and D. Goswami (eds), *Writing in Nonacademic Settings*. New York: Guilford Press, pp. 205–29.

Murray, D. E. (1986) Computer-mediated communication as an instructional tool. In Oliver Seely Jr. (ed.), *Tenth Western Educational Computing Conference*. North Hollywood, CA: CECC, pp. 41–5.

Murray, D. E. (1988a) Computer-mediated communication: implications for ESP. *English for Specific Purposes*, 7, 3–18.

Murray, D. E. (1988b) The context of oral and written language: a framework for mode and medium switching. *Language in Society*, 17, 351–73.

Murray, D. E. (1988c) Orality and literacy in the computer age. *ACH Newsletter*, 10, 1, 14–15.

Murray, D. E. (1988d) Computer-mediated communication in IBM. *Technical Communication*, October, 339–40.

Murray, D. E. (1989) When the medium determines turns: turn-taking in computer conversation. In H. Coleman (eds.), *Working with Language*. The Hague: Mouton, pp. 210–23.

Murray, D. E. (1990) Literacies as sociocultural phenomena. *Prospect*, 6, 55–62.

Murray, D. E. (1991) *Conversation for Action: The computer Terminal as Medium of Communication*. The Hague: John Benjamins.

Newell, A. and Sproull, R. F. (1982) Computer networks: prospects for scientists. *International Journal of Man-Machine Studies*, 17, 375–99.

Norman, D. A. (1988) *The Psychology of Everyday Things*. New York: Basic Books.

Obermeier, K. K. (1989) *Natural Language Processing Technologies in Artificial Intelligence*. New York: Ellis Horwood.

Oberst, D. and Smith, S. (1986) BITNET: Past, present and future. *Educom Bulletin*, 21, 10–16.

Ochwat, J. (1994) Reporters, who needs reporters? *San José Mercury News*, 8 May, 1F, 6F, 7F.

Ong, W. (1977) *Interfaces of the Word: Studies in the Evolution of Consciousness and Culture*. Ithaca NY: Cornell University Press.

Ong, W. J. (1982) *Orality and Literacy: The Technologizing of the Word*. London: Methuen.

Pankoke-Babtz, U. (ed.) (1989) *Computer-Based Group Communication: The AMIGO model*. Chichester: Ellis Horwood.

Pattison, R. (1982) *On Literacy*. Oxford: Oxford University Press.

Philips, S. U. (1983) *The Invisible Culture*. New York: Longman.

Plotnikoff, D. (1994) System overload. *San José Mercury News*, 5 April, 1C, 5C.

Quartermann, J. and Hoskins, J. (1986) Notable computer networks. *Communications of the ACM*, 29, 932–71.

Reingold, E. (1990) Facing the `Totally New and Dynamic'. *Time*, 6–7.

Rotenberg, M. (1993) Prepared Testimony and Statement for the Record of Marc Rotenberg, Director, CPSR Washington Office, Adjunct Professor, Georgetown University Law Center on H.R. 1900, The Privacy for Consumers and Workers Act Before The Subcommittee on Labor-Management Relations, Committee on Education and Labor, US House of Representatives, 30 June.

Rubenstein, R. and Hersch, H. (1984) *The Human Factor: Designing Computer Systems for People*. Burlington, Mass.: Digital Press.

Sachs, S. (1987) Minitel chat lines seduce French with technology. *San José Mercury News*, 4 October 1A, 6A.

Sacks, H., Schegloff, E. and Jefferson, G. (1974) A simplest systematics for the organization of turn-taking for conversation. *Language*, 50, 4, 696–735.

Sandler, C. (1986) *How to Telecommunicate: A Personal Computer User's Guide*. New York: Henry Holt & Company.

Scarola, R. (1986) Kids are discovering electronic pen pals. *San José Mercury News*, 26 October 1F, 6F.

Schank, R. and Abelson, R. (1977) *Scripts, Plans, Goals and Understanding*. Hillsdale, NJ: Erlbaum.

Schegloff, E. (1972) Note on conversational practice: formulating place. In P. P. Giglioli (eds), *Language and Social Context*. Harmondsworth, Middlesex: Penguin, pp. 95–135.

Schegloff, E. (1976) Identification and recognition in telephone conversation openings. In G. Psathas (eds), *Everyday Language: Studies in Ethnomethodology*. New York: Irvington, pp. 23–78.

Schegloff, E. and Sacks, H. (1973) Opening up closings. *Semiotica*, 7, 4, 289–327.

Schegloff, E., Jefferson, G. and Sacks, H. (1977) The preference for self-correction in the organization of repair in conversation. *Language*, 53, 361–82.

Searle, J. (1980) Minds, brains and programs. *Behavioral and Brain Science*, 3, 417–57.

Searle, J. (1976) The classification of illocutionary acts. *Language in Society*, 5, 1–24.

Siegel, J., Dubrovsky, V., Kiesler, S. and McGuire, T. (1986) Group processes in computer-mediated communication. *Organizational Behavior and Human Decision Processes*, 37, 157–87.

Simons, G. (1987) *Eco-Computer: The Impact of Global Intelligence*. Chichester: John Wiley & Sons.

Simpson, B. (1984) Heading for the Ha-Ha. In Douglas Sloan (ed.), *The Computer in Education: A Critical Perspective*. New York: Teachers College Press.

Sloan, D. (ed.) (1984) *The Computer in Education: A Critical Perspective*. New York: Teachers College Press.

Sproull, L. and Kiesler, S. (1986) Reducing social context cues: the case of electronic mail. *Management Science*, 32, 1492–512.

Stober, D. (1989) The hacker tracker. *San José Mercury News*, 20 March, 7B, 8B.

Stoll, C. (1989) *The Cuckoo's Egg: Tracking a Spy Through the Maze of Computer Espionage*. New York: Doubleday.

Straumann, H. (1935) *Newspaper Headlines: A Study in Linguistic Method*. London: Allen and Unwin.

Street, B. (1984) *Literacy in Theory and Practice*. Cambridge: Cambridge University Press.

Tannen, D. (1982) The oral-literate continuum in discourse. In D. Tannen (ed.), *Spoken and Written Language: Exploring Orality and Literacy*. Norwood, NJ: Ablex, pp. 1–16.

Teichman, M. and Poris, M. (1989) Initial effects of word processing on writing quality and writing anxiety of freshman writers. *Computers and the Humanities*, 23, 2, 93–103.

Toffler, A. (1992) *War and Anti-War*. New York: Littlebrown.

Tombaugh, J. (1984) Evaluation of an international scientific computer-based conference. *Journal of Social Issues*, 40, 3, 129–44.

Turkle, S. (1984) *The Second Self: Computers and the Human Spirit*. New York: Simon and Schuster.

Unger, M. J. (1987) *The Fifth Generation Fallacy: Why Japan is Betting the Future on Artificial Intelligence*. Oxford: Oxford University Press.

Updegrove, D. A., Muffo, J. A. and Dunn, J. (1990) Electronic mail and networks: new tools for university administrators. *Cause/Effect*, 13, 41–8.

Ventola, E. (1983) Contrasting schematic structures in service encounters. *Applied Linguistics*, 4, 8, 242–58.

Wallace, A. (1992) Bulletin board brought light in LA's dark hour. *San José Mercury News*, 15 July, 8E, 15E.

Walsh, B. P., Butcher, H. and Freund, A. (1987) *On-line Information: A Comprehensive Business User's Guide*. London: Basil Blackwell.

Wilkins, H. (1991) Computer talk: long-distance conversations by computer. *Written Communication*, 8, 1, 56–78.

Windt, J. (1983) Minding your on-line manners. *San José Mercury News*, 30 November, 1D, 2D.

Winograd, T. and Flores, F. (1986) *Understanding Computers and Cognition*. Norwood, NJ: Ablex.

Winograd, T. (1984) Computer software for working with language. *Scientific American*, September, 131–45.

Woodbury, M. (1994) A quick look at the costs and benefits of computers in Higher Education. *The CPSR Newsletter*, Spring, 15–19.

Yule, G. (1985) *The Study of Language*. Cambridge: Cambridge University Press.

Index